See You in Court

of related interest

Handbook for Practice Learning in Social Work and Social Care
Knowledge and Theory
Edited by Joyce Lishman
ISBN 978 1 84310 186 4

The Post-Qualifying Handbook for Social Workers
Edited by Wade Tovey
ISBN 978 1 84310 428 5

Competence in Social Work Practice
A Practical Guide for Students and Professionals
Edited by Kieran O'Hagan
ISBN 978 1 84310 485 8

Domestic Violence and Child Protection
Directions for Good Practice
Edited by Cathy Humphreys and Nicky Stanley
ISBN 978 1 84310 276 2

Child Protection, Domestic Violence and Parental Substance Misuse
Family Experiences and Effective Practice
Hedy Cleaver, Don Nicholson, Sukey Tarr and Deborah Cleaver
ISBN 978 1 84310 582 4

The Nearest Relative Handbook
David Hewitt
ISBN 978 1 84310 522 0

Developments in Social Work with Offenders
Edited by Gill McIvor and Peter Raynor
ISBN 978 1 84310 538 1

Residential Child Care
Prospects and Challenges
Edited by Andrew Kendrick
ISBN 978 1 84310 526 8

Youth Justice and Child Protection
Edited by Malcolm Hill, Andrew Lockyer and Fred Stone
ISBN 978 1 84310 279 3

See You in Court

A Social Worker's Guide to Presenting Evidence in Care Proceedings

Lynn Davis

Jessica Kingsley Publishers
London and Philadelphia

First published in 2007
by Jessica Kingsley Publishers
116 Pentonville Road
London N1 9JB, UK
and
400 Market Street, Suite 400
Philadelphia, PA 19106, USA

www.jkp.com

Library of Congress Cataloging in Publication Data
Davis, Lynn.
See you in court : a social worker's guide to presenting evidence in care proceedings / Lynn
Davis.
p. cm.
Includes bibliographical references.
ISBN-13: 978-1-84310-547-3 (pb : alk. paper) 1. Domestic relations courts--Great
Britain. 2. Social courts--Great Britain. 3. Evidence, Expert--Great Britain. 4. Social
workers--Legal status, laws, etc.--Great Britain. I. Title.
KD751.D38 2007
344.7303'13--dc22

2007013575

British Library Cataloguing in Publication Data
A CIP catalogue record for this book is available from the British Library

ISBN 978 1 84310 547 3

Printed and bound in Great Britain by
Athenaeum Press, Gateshead, Tyne and Wear

Contents

List of figures, tables and boxes

List of scenarios

Acknowledgments

Extracts from reported cases are reproduced by kind permission of Jordan Publishing, publishers of the indispensable Family Law Reports.

I am grateful to His Honour Judge Murdoch QC, Malcolm Dodds, John Emery and Debbie Aston for their helpful suggestions, to my friend and colleague Christopher Simmonds for his comments on the manuscript, to Louisa Penman and Perry Murphy for researching case references, to Celia Morris and Stuart Fuller for their help on court skills courses and to my editor, Steve Jones, for guiding me through the publishing process. I am also indebted to my former clients and the child care lawyers, social workers and Children's Guardians of Kent and Medway for all they have taught me over the years.

Thanks too to Mark and the pack for their help, patience and encouragement.

This book is dedicated to Mum and Dad with grateful thanks for a lifetime of love and support.

Preface

This book is the result of 15 years' experience of care proceedings divided almost equally between acting for the local authority and for respondents, both parents and children (on direct instructions or via their Children's Guardians). It attempts to answer questions raised by social workers during real cases and court skills training courses. I hope it will be useful.

It is about the process of care proceedings rather than child care law and so is no substitute for expert legal advice on any particular case. Where the law is referred to, it is up to date as at 1 May 2007, so please be alert to the possibility of any subsequent changes.

Throughout the book, to avoid repetition of he/she, one gender or the other has been chosen. Lawyers are assumed to be male; social workers are assumed to be female. Of course no offence is intended to female lawyers or male social workers. Similarly the law of England and Wales is sometimes referred to simply as English law, and no disrespect is intended towards Welsh colleagues.

Any opinions expressed are entirely my own and I take full responsibility for, and apologise for, any mistakes.

Chapter 1

Introduction

Expectations and preconceptions

Are you looking forward to going to court? Or does the very thought inspire dread? Like it or not, as a children and families social worker, you will one day end up in the witness box. You owe it to yourself (not to mention your clients) to prepare yourself as well as possible, so you can approach the experience with well-founded confidence and perform your role effectively.

Many fears about court are based on unjustified preconceptions. Courts in real life bear little resemblance to TV dramas, most of which are set in criminal courts, which are very different in approach from family courts, and many of which are American. In the UK advocates are not allowed to stroll around the courtroom eyeballing the witness or the jury, and rarely jump up shouting 'objection'. Sadly, few advocates look like Hollywood actors, and cases seldom turn on last minute surprise revelations.

Social workers facing their first experience of proceedings can be pessimistic, even fearful of court and may expect disaster. As with anything else in life, a negative starting attitude is likely to become a self-fulfilling prophecy. Expectations of problems are often fuelled by tales of difficulties experienced by others. Usually these have been grossly magnified on the grapevine, and only represent a tiny proportion of cases – 'everything went fine' is not news, 'it was a nightmare' is. Try to base your ideas on reality, not on exaggerated reports.

Why do court proceedings inspire such foreboding?

Fear of the unknown

Imagine asking someone who had never even been to the theatre to step straight onto the stage and perform in a play. Surely that would be a ridiculous idea, leading inevitably to embarrassment and disaster. Yet social workers routinely seem to be expected to give evidence the first time they ever set foot in a courtroom. Being thrown in the deep end is not usually the best way to learn to swim.

Being an effective witness is a skill which can be learned. Don't assume that it should come naturally. Excellent witnesses make it all look easy – but that is usually because they have worked hard at it.

Fear of the unknown is a normal emotion. New steps, especially important ones where you are taking responsibility for serious actions and where you feel all eyes are upon you, naturally cause apprehension. The key is to make sure you are as well prepared and supported as possible throughout the process.

Remember that the final court hearing is far from the whole story. In fact, it is only the culmination of a long process which starts with social work, a skill you already possess. Any children and families case could end up in court, so it is sensible to approach all your cases on the assumption that one day you will be explaining the case and your actions to the court. That way, you ensure that every case is well recorded, decisions clearly evidenced, procedures followed, inter-agency co-operation secured and supervision sought. Your court case is then based on solid foundations. The rest of the process essentially consists of explaining to the court the social work you have done and your department's decisions, first in writing then orally in court. The new skills to learn relate only to the rules and etiquette of the presentation to this new forum but, if your work is sound, the content is already there.

This book aims to help you understand the context of court work and the details of court proceedings, particularly in care cases. In addition, take up any training on offer and make sure you benefit as much as possible from your colleagues' experience. Find people who have had a good experience of court or who are known as effective witnesses (your legal department may have suggestions) and talk to them. There is nothing like first-hand experience.

Don't sit back and wait for others to help you – you are not likely to be top of their list of priorities. Don't wait until you know your case is going to court – that will be too late. Get the help you need to do your job; ask and remind – insist if necessary.

Read as many court statements and reports as you can before you have to write one yourself. Don't assume, however, that they are all well written. Read them critically, noting what comes over well and what does not.

Go to court as an observer before you ever have to go as a witness. Family courts are currently held in private[1] but judges and magistrates are usually happy to allow one or two professionals to observe proceedings for training

---

1   Department of Constitutional Affairs (2006) *Confidence and Confidentiality: Improving Transparency and Privacy in Family Courts (CP 11/06)*. London: Department of Constitutional Affairs. Accessed on 1/5/07 at http://www.dca.gov.uk/consult/courttransparencey1106/consultation1106.pdf. The responses to the consultation were published on 22 March 2007 and can be accessed (as at 1/5/07) at http://www.dca.gov.uk/consult/courttransparencey1106/response-cp1106.pdf.

purposes. Ask your colleagues or your legal advisers to let you know when a suitable case for you to observe is taking place.

Whenever you are in court, be it the first or the hundredth time, watch and learn. Courts vary, and every day is different; there is always something new to absorb. What is each person's role in the process? Why are they doing what they are doing? How well are they performing their role? How effective is each witness, and why? Look out for impressive witnesses and analyse what makes them persuasive – see what you can learn from them. If a witness is not so compelling, consider what made you form this view, and ask yourself what would have been more effective? How is the court reacting to what is being said – in short, what works?

Formality

The stereotypical social worker has an informal approach to life and does not welcome the constraints of formality. Like all stereotypes this may contain an element of truth, but it is far from the whole picture and you are already well used to formal occasions where there are rules of procedure and behaviour. It can even be quite comforting to know what is expected of you.

It is true that court is a rather traditional, conservative, formal affair, although far less so in the family jurisdiction than other types of court. However, as a matter of principle, it must be right that the formality of court should reflect the gravity of the decisions being taken. As long as you follow the rules and conform to the court's expectations, you can get the job done for your child client. You will learn to find your own 'witness' persona – still yourself, but a particular version of yourself.

Artificiality

Sometimes social workers feel dissatisfied with the artificiality and theatricality of the trial system. They see advocates apparently fighting each other in court, then leaving the building chatting amicably, or they see the same lawyer arguing completely contradictory cases with equal vigour from one day to the next. They suspect that the advocates often say things they do not really believe, and this seems dishonest. It all seems like a game.

An important key to coping with the court process is understanding how the system works and what roles the other participants play, putting yourself in their shoes. The advocate is simply an expert mouthpiece for his client. It has been said that an advocate is like a hired gun – he shoots who he is paid to shoot and his own feelings or beliefs do not come into it. It is not a game, it is a job, and a very serious one at that.

It may be that if we were starting from scratch to design a system to determine children's futures it would not look much like our current one. No one pretends that our system is ideal. However, wishing it were different is like the joke response to a request for directions 'well, I wouldn't start from here'. The fact is that, imperfect as it may be, this is the only system we have got, and we have to work within it.

Confrontation

We are all exhorted to work in partnership with parents and as a social worker you no doubt spend a lot of time trying to secure everyone's co-operation for the sake of the child. It can seem contradictory then to have to bring the case to the adversarial setting of the court where you and the parents are on opposing 'sides'.

In other cases you may have been walking a tightrope trying to secure the co-operation of a difficult family and fear that confrontation will jeopardise any chances of progress, or even the child's safety. However, parental hostility is never a reason to fail to take proceedings, indeed it may strengthen the need to take the case into the court arena.

By taking proceedings, you inevitably bring matters to a head. Concerns have to be spelled out and evidenced in formal documentation, perhaps more starkly than before, but nothing you put in evidence should come as a surprise to the family. In your work with them you should already have been clear about the reasons for your involvement, what has to change, why and how. A Child Protection Case Conference may already have formally expressed multi-agency concerns and set a programme for change. If you have not clearly communicated the issues before taking the case to court, expect to have to explain why not.

Family court cases are supposed to be heard in a non-adversarial atmosphere. Being explicit about what has happened and what has to change does not require unnecessary antagonism, at least not on the part of the local authority. Do not feel you have to put aside your professional ethos of compassion and respect at the court door and remember that when the case is over you still need to find a way of working with the parents and child.

In the future, there may be other ways of resolving family disputes, but for the time being there are some matters, such as making a care order, which lie exclusively in the power of the court. When co-operation and partnership have failed to achieve a child's protection, there is no alternative but to move to another forum and take the case to court.

Responsibility

It can be a daunting prospect to be the key worker taking care proceedings. However, remember that you are not alone. It is the local authority which takes proceedings, not you as an individual, and many others are involved in any court case including your lawyers and people from other agencies.

In proceedings you are the representative of the local authority, and are of course constrained by its procedures and policies. You need to be clearly aware of the extent of and limitations to your capacity for action and how far you can or cannot make decisions to bind the authority. In return you are protected by employment legislation, so your health and safety, for example, are your employer's concern, and the local authority is vicariously liable for any actions you take in the course of your employment, even if you are negligent. That is not to say, of course, that you can escape responsibility for your actions, which might have legal or disciplinary consequences. You also have to sleep at night. The key thing to remember is that in child protection, whether in court or outside, no action should be casual and no remark made lightly. If you think through whatever you do, say or decide not to do, even if others later disagree with your judgement, you can at least explain yourself.

It is vital to ensure that all care proceedings are a team effort, including multi-agency co-operation and close liaison with your legal representatives. The fact is that child protection is an art not a science. If you were looking for an easy life, you would not have chosen to work in child protection. Dr Julia Brophy's survey of research indicates that care proceedings cases are complex and only serious cases are brought to court.[2] Most involve more than one category of child abuse or neglect as well as several different areas of concern about the parents, often including failure to co-operate with professionals.

As Lord Nicholls said in the House of Lords case of *Re H and R*[3]:

> The task of social workers is usually anxious and often thankless. They are criticised for not having taken action in response to warning signs which are obvious enough when seen in the clear light of hindsight. Or they are criticised for making applications based on serious allegations which, in the event, are not established in court. Sometimes, whatever they do, they cannot do right.

As a social worker, you are a member of a profession which constantly struggles to establish its credibility. There is still a perception that social workers lack skill and professionalism, sometimes leading to an independent expert being instructed in proceedings to do little more than validate the social worker's

2   Brophy, J. (2006) Research Review. *Child Care Proceedings under the Children Act 1989*. London: Department of Constitutional Affairs. Accessed on 1/5/2007 at http://www.dca.gov.uk/research/2006/05_2006.htm.

3   *Re H & R (Child sexual abuse: standard of proof)* [1996] 1FLR 80, House of Lords, p.101 G–H.

assessment. You owe it to yourself and your profession to challenge that perception by the quality of your work and your presentation. Only by consistently demonstrating that the courts can trust them will social workers achieve the respect they deserve.

Positives

Some social workers positively enjoy going to court and many others take this part of their role in their stride. Preparing a case and taking it to court is a stimulating intellectual challenge. It involves the rigorous analysis of facts set against legal criteria. You have the opportunity to explain and justify your professional judgement to an independent adjudicator, while countering challenges and objections. It gives you the opportunity for authoritative validation of your practice and your department's planning for the child. Often judges and magistrates comment on the work undertaken or evidence given and this can include compliments on the quality of social work witnesses. It is another step in your professional development, and achieving another milestone should be satisfying, especially if it involves overcoming difficulties on the way.

Only the court can move matters along for the child by making necessary orders, and it must be right as a matter of principle that these vital decisions should only be made after due process. The parents and the child himself, whether immediately if he is old enough or later when he is trying to understand his life story, have the right to know that the case has been properly scrutinised and tested.

At the end of the process, achieving the right outcome for the child makes all the difficulties along the way worthwhile.

QUESTIONS FOR REFLECTION

- How do you feel about court work? Why?
- What do you need to do to prepare yourself?

Chapter 2

The Legal Context

The adversarial system

The English legal system follows an adversarial model. As the name suggests, it is based on the idea of two adversaries battling it out, with the court hearing both sides and determining the victor. The court does not actively participate in the contest except to regulate its conduct, in the role of referee, enforcing the rules during proceedings and then acting as adjudicator. Just as a referee does not interfere in the competitors' choice of tactics or techniques, the court does not dictate how the respective parties put their case – it is up to them to present their cases as they think fit, putting forward their own evidence and deciding on their own arguments. The court takes an essentially passive role; it is dependent on the information brought to it by the parties themselves. This is quite unlike a continental-style inquisitorial system where a court officer directs enquiries and has an active role in determining the information the court takes into account in its decision.

Remember, therefore, that the court is dependent on you – it has no independent knowledge. The judge or magistrates do not meet the child, visit the family home or see the parents interact with the child. It is up to you to convey all the relevant information: if you do not tell the court something, it will not know about it. Remembering this will help you decide what information to include in your evidence. Also bear in mind that the judge is not a social worker and does not have the same skills as you do, for example, in interpreting family dynamics. At times, therefore, as well as giving the court information, you also need to bring to the court the benefit of your expertise.

It is often said that Children Act proceedings are 'non-adversarial', but this refers to the atmosphere of the court and the less antagonistic approach of the advocates rather than the system itself, which remains fundamentally an adversarial model.

Court hierarchy

Courts are organised in a hierarchy, as illustrated in Figure 2.1, and those at the bottom of the chart are the workhorses of the system. The magistrates' court has an important jurisdiction in both criminal and family law. All criminal cases start there, for both adults and (in the Youth Court) juveniles, and while serious cases are committed to the Crown Court, magistrates deal with 90 per cent of criminal cases from start to finish.

The Family Proceedings Court (FPC) is part of the magistrates' court. Care proceedings start in the FPC apart from a few exceptions, such as where another case about the same child is already underway in a higher court. Cases can stay in the FPC throughout or be transferred up to a County Court which is designated as a Care Centre (that is, a County Court which is designated to undertake public law children's work) and, if necessary, from there on to the High Court. The grounds for transfer are that the case is of exceptional gravity, complexity or length, so that each case is heard in the appropriate level of court. Thus a case of general neglect – inadequate food, poor hygiene and so on – might be ideal for the FPC, but a case of an allegedly non-accidental head injury would go up to the County Court and perhaps to the High Court if, for example, experts held conflicting views. The Courts Service plans to introduce unified family court centres, so a transfer to a different level of court will no longer mean moving to a different building. This should streamline administration, increase efficiency and, it is hoped, create a more family-centred atmosphere.

At the end of a trial, when the court's decision is announced, the unsuccessful party may wish to appeal. However, dissatisfaction with the court's decision is not in itself enough to give grounds for appeal – the aggrieved party must establish that the court which made the initial decision (known as the 'court of first instance') made a mistake of law, or applied the law wrongly to the facts of the case.

The High Court has a dual role in care proceedings, being both a court of first instance, hearing very complicated cases, and an appellate court, hearing appeals from the FPC. Above the High Court in the hierarchy, the Court Appeal and House of Lords have an exclusively appellate jurisdiction. They do not re-hear evidence, so no witnesses are called; instead they work from transcripts of the evidence and judgments given in the court below, and hear arguments on points of law. If one of your cases goes to appeal, you will not have to give evidence, so your role is limited to helping your legal team to put the case as clearly and forcefully as possible.

The House of Lords only hears cases raising an issue of general public importance, of significance far beyond the interests of the parties involved. This totals less than a hundred cases a year over the whole range of law, so very few children's cases proceed to this level.

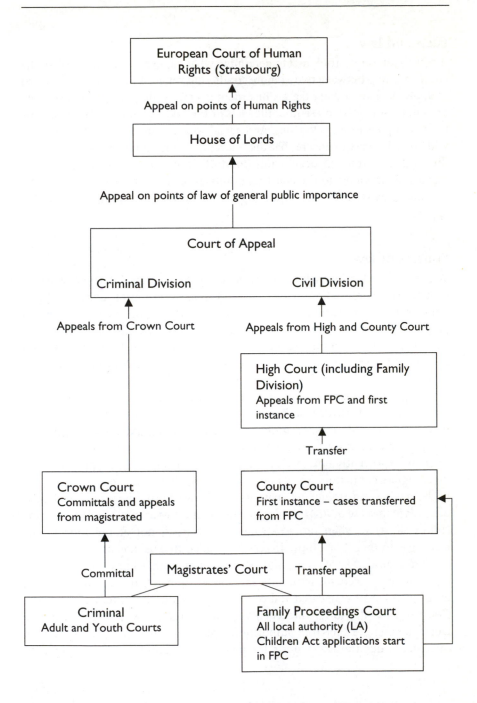

Figure 2.1: Court hierarchy in England and Wales

Facts and law

A court's job is two-fold; first to determine what happened, which involves the court choosing between two or more conflicting versions of events, and second to apply the law to those facts. Constructing a care proceedings case therefore does not just involve presenting the facts of the case but also establishing how the law applies to that evidence. As a social worker, you need to work closely with your lawyers to ensure that the relevant legal grounds are established by the evidence. Your advocate's job (for full details see Chapter 3) includes making submissions to the court on points of legal interpretation and, if the decision goes against you, considering whether there are any legal grounds for appeal.

Sources of law

You should be familiar with statutes such as the Children Act 1989, which is central to care proceedings. However, English law is not just founded on legislation but also on case law. Some important doctrines of our law are purely judge-made common law such as the law of negligence, the cause of today's concerns about a 'compensation culture', which all stems from the case of a decomposing snail found in a bottle of ginger beer (*Donoghue v Stevenson* 1932).[1]

Judges also interpret statutes to decide on the precise meaning of the words used in an Act of Parliament. For example, s31 Children Act 1989 defines the so-called 'threshold criteria' grounds for a care or supervision order. Almost every word of that section has been subject to judicial scrutiny, including the small and apparently unremarkable word 'is' in the phrase 'the child is suffering…significant harm…'. You might think that what 'is' means is obvious, but nothing is beyond argument to lawyers. The issue went all the way to the House of Lords in the case of *Re M*,[2] which decided that the court must look back at the child's situation when protective measures started, not at the time of the hearing – so their Lordships effectively decided that 'is' means 'was'.

The House of Lords is the highest court in the land, so its decisions constitute 'binding precedent' setting the law for all other courts. Thus the meaning of 'is' in s31 is now decided and is not open to any other interpretation. The Court of Appeal also sets precedents for all courts below it in the hierarchy. Decided cases are therefore authority for propositions of law, so lawyers on each side scour the law reports for precedents supporting their arguments.

1   *Donoghue v Stevenson* [1932] AC 562.

2   *Re M (a minor) (Care order: threshold criteria)* [1994] 2FLR 557, House of Lords.

They also try to undermine the arguments put forward by the opposition by contending, for example, that a case does not apply because a distinction can be drawn between the case cited as a precedent and the matter before the court. Lawyers usually put their legal arguments in written submissions or skeleton arguments. If you are the key worker in a case, always ask to see your own advocate's written submissions before they are handed in, so you can see how your case is put. You should also see the other parties' arguments as soon as they are received.

Another key consideration for all courts is the Human Rights Act 1998, and case law from the European Court of Human Rights in Strasbourg is now regularly cited in our own courts. Human rights issues include the right to family life, right to a fair hearing and the right to protection from ill-treatment, so you can expect these to be raised in all of your cases.

Criminal and civil law

In the English legal system, cases are categorised as either criminal or civil. The function of the criminal law is to define and mark the limit of acceptable behaviour in society and an individual who steps beyond that boundary is subject to the censure of the State. For this reason, prosecutions are taken in the name of the Crown, so a case against Mr Smith is called *R* (which stands for Regina) *v Smith*, and the prosecuting authority is the Crown Prosecution Service. The spotlight of a criminal case falls on the behaviour of a particular person, the defendant, and the State's job is to establish whether this individual has transgressed against a specified law, and to convict and punish or to acquit him.

Criminal offences are tightly defined and the prosecution must establish that each element of the offence was committed by the particular defendant on trial. He, of course, is innocent until proved guilty, an ancient protection for the individual now also enshrined in the European Convention on Human Rights. The burden placed on the prosecution is a heavy one – proof beyond reasonable doubt is required – and the rules of evidence are strict. As a matter of principle, it is generally thought better that a guilty man go free than an innocent man be convicted.

Lay people play a vital role in the criminal courts. Most cases are tried by magistrates who have no legal qualifications. In the Crown Court, where serious crimes are tried, the verdict of guilty or not guilty is given by a jury of lay people. These roles for 'ordinary people' reflect the fact that the criminal law is there to impose and enforce society's norms. This is reinforced by the fact that, except for cases against juveniles, criminal trials are open to press and public so that justice can be seen to be done.

Civil law, on the other hand, primarily deals with resolving disputes between individuals. Although care proceedings are classed as public law as the applicant is the local authority, an arm of the State, they still fall within the court's civil jurisdiction.

Civil courts from the Small Claims Court (part of the County Court) to the High Court are occupied with matters such as negligence claims, contract disputes and, of course, family law. Issues tend to be broader than the tightly defined offences before the criminal courts.

The court's objective in a civil case is to resolve the dispute by making findings of fact and determining rights and duties between individuals. The court then finds a suitable solution to the problem, be it compensation, an injunction or, in family cases, an order regulating arrangements such as a residence or contact order. Even if the court does make findings of fact (for example, that Mr Bloggs sexually abused the child), these do not have the same force or status as a criminal conviction and do not lead, for example, to entry on the sex offenders register.

As a result of the civil law's function it is not necessary, nor would it be practical, for matters to be proved to the same level as a criminal case. The applicant has to establish his case 'on the balance of probabilities' that is to say to show that his case is more likely than not to be the correct one. It is important to be keenly aware of the difference between the criminal and civil standards of proof. If these were to be expressed in numerical terms, where would you place each standard on a scale of 1 to 100, where 50 is evenly balanced?

Clearly the criminal standard is high, although the word 'reasonable' means that the prosecution does not have to prove its case beyond any doubt at all; 100 per cent certainty is impossible in the real world. Police officers generally put the figure at around the 90 per cent mark; still a very high level of proof. In contrast, the civil standard might technically correctly be expressed as 51 per cent – in theory anything above 50 per cent reaches the target. However, in practice such small differences are impossible to detect and civil lawyers tend to express the figure as more like 60 per cent. The gap between the two standards is striking; proof at a level of 75 per cent, for example, would be ample to satisfy the civil standard but nowhere approaching the criminal standard.

Terminology

You need to be very clear whether you are working in the criminal or civil arena, and to adjust your approach and use the correct terminology accordingly. For example, the term 'prosecution' is only used in the criminal courts – to use it in care proceedings would reveal a misunderstanding and demonstrate a completely inappropriate mindset. Some differences are more subtle, for example, what we would call in the criminal context a 'confession' becomes an 'admission' in the civil court.

Children's cases

Child protection cases can give rise to both criminal and civil proceedings, meaning that as a social worker you may be required to give evidence in both the family and the criminal courts. Although the same basic facts lead to both court cases, your role changes from applicant in the former to witness in the latter, the respective courts vary in focus, function and approach and the potential outcomes are quite different in nature.

Scenarios

Scenario 2.1: Sexual abuse: crime and care

Amy, aged 8, says her stepfather Barry sexually assaulted her. Police and Social Services investigate, making a video-recorded interview conducted under the 'Achieving Best Evidence'[3] guidelines. Professionals agree that Amy's disclosure is clear. Barry is arrested, charged with indecent assault and taken before the criminal court. Amy's mother, Carrie, refuses to believe the allegations and supports her husband. Social Services start care proceedings to remove Amy from home.

Two separate court cases are underway. The criminal court focuses on Barry and the alleged offence; the family court focuses on Amy's welfare, looking at her whole circumstances, not just the issue of sexual abuse. In the criminal case, Amy has to go to court to be cross-examined, albeit by live TV link. In the care proceedings, professionals give Amy's evidence for her, and she is extremely unlikely to have to go to court herself.

The evidence against Barry is not strong enough to sustain a conviction for sexual assault and he is acquitted of criminal charges, but in the care proceedings court the judge makes a finding that he did indeed sexually abuse Amy.

QUESTIONS FOR REFLECTION

• How can Barry make sense of his situation? As far as he is concerned, he has been found innocent by one court but condemned by another.

• How can you explain the situation to Amy?

---

3   Home Office Communications Directorate (2002) *Achieving Best Evidence in Criminal Proceedings: Guidance for Vulnerable or Intimidated Witnesses, Including Children.* London: Home Office. Accessed on 1/5/07 at http://www.homeoffice.gov.uk/documents/ achieving-best-evidence/.

Table 2.1 summarises some differences between the two sets of proceedings.

Table 2.1 Differences between criminal and care proceedings

	Criminal	Care
Parties	Crown (prosecution) Barry (defendant)	Local authority (applicant) Carrie, Amy's father (if he has parental responsibility), Amy (via her Children's Guardian) (respondents) [Note: Barry, as Amy's stepfather, is not automatically a party]
Court	Start in Magistrates' Court, committal to Crown Court	Start in FPC, transfer to County Court
Decision-maker	Crown Court – jury decides facts	County Court judge
Privacy?	No – Crown Court open to public and press	Yes – only parties in court[4]
Burden of proof	Prosecution	Applicant
Standard of proof	Beyond reasonable doubt	Balance of probabilities
Evidential rules	Very strict	Less strict
Relevant evidence	Alleged offence only	Amy's whole circumstances, not just alleged abuse
Amy's evidence	Amy gives evidence via video and TV link	Video shown; interviewers give evidence; Amy extremely unlikely to come to court
Amy's status	Victim/witness	Subject of proceedings
Focus on	Barry	Amy

---

4   Department of Constitutional Affairs (2006) *Confidence and Confidentiality: Improving Transparency and Privacy in family courts* (CP 11/106). London: Department of Constitutional Affairs. Accessed on 1/5/07 at http://www.dca.gov.uk/consult/courttransparencey1106/consultation1106.pdf.

Table 2.1 *cont.*

	Criminal	Care
Dress	Judge and advocates wear wigs and gowns	No wigs or gowns
Tone	Adversarial	Non-adversarial
Outcome	Verdict – guilty/not guilty	Decision/judgment – findings of fact
	Punishment if convicted	Order or no order – resolution of Amy's situation
Purpose	To determine Barry's guilt or innocence	To determine Amy's best interests

---

Scenario 2.2: Out of control: crime and care

Donna is 14 and out of control. She truants from school, takes drugs, drinks to excess and is promiscuous. She steals to finance her drug habit. Donna is arrested, charged and prosecuted in the Youth Court for theft. She is also subject to care proceedings as she is suffering significant harm because of her own behaviour and is beyond parental control.

Both cases centre on Donna, but the criminal case concerns only on her alleged criminal offences – the underlying causes and her other problems only become relevant if she is convicted and the court has to consider what sentence to impose. In contrast, the whole focus of the care proceedings is whether Donna is suffering significant harm and her welfare is the court's paramount consideration. In the Youth Court, Donna is the object of censure; in the family court she is the subject of concern.

QUESTION FOR REFLECTION

- How can you help Donna to understand why her behaviour is condemned by one court and the subject of concern for the other?

Scenario 2.3: Child death: crime and care

Edward dies from physical injuries and medical opinion is clear that these were non-accidental. Evidence shows they occurred when Edward was in the care of both parents. They deny doing, seeing or hearing anything untoward but have no explanation for the injuries. There are no other witnesses to what occurred. The evidence cannot establish who is responsible for Edward's death. What implications does this have for the criminal and family courts?

Edward has been killed; you might think a murder or manslaughter charge should follow. But this scenario presents an impossible dilemma for the criminal law: who can be charged? There are two suspects equally in the frame and no evidence to establish which of them was responsible – if both continue to deny everything and no other evidence is discovered, there is no hope of proving beyond reasonable doubt who killed Edward. Criminal law requires a defendant – two people cannot be prosecuted on an 'either/or' basis. The police might arrest and interview both parents in the hope of evidence coming to light, and might consider lesser charges relating to failure to seek medical attention, but the chances are that no one will be prosecuted for killing Edward.

For the family court it is clearly too late for Edward, but his baby brother Fred may be in grave danger. The evidence of Edward's injuries can be presented to court to establish the likelihood of significant harm to Fred, attributable to his parents' behaviour. The focus is on Fred's welfare, and the fact that neither parent can be singled out as his brother's killer does not prevent the grounds for a care order being established. This important principle was confirmed by the House of Lords in the case Re O and N (minors) and Re B (minors).[5]

QUESTIONS FOR REFLECTION

- You have protected Fred, but how do you feel about the fact that no one is prosecuted for Edward's death?
- How does this affect your ongoing work with the family?
- How will you explain it to Fred when he is old enough to understand?

5   Re O & N (minors) and Re B (minors) [2003] 1 FLR 1169, House of Lords.

Hedley J gave a lucid analysis of the differences between criminal and family hearings in the care proceedings case of *A Local Authority v S, W & T*[6] where a father had been acquitted in the Crown Court of murdering one of his children. Hedley J explained that the acquittal meant that the jury:

> decided that they were not sure: no more than that can be read into the verdict. They may have decided that he was in fact innocent or they may have decided that he was very probably guilty but that they could not be sure of it. We do not know. ...In family proceedings, however, the judge's task is quite different. In the end I will have to decide whether the surviving child T can be safely returned to one or both of her parents. In order to decide that, I need to reach views about why X died and the question I have to ask is this: what was the most probable cause of her death? That is very different to the question faced by the jury both in terms of its emphasis (they were primarily concerned with W as the defendant whilst I am primarily concerned with the child) and in terms of the standard of proof. They had to be sure of guilt; I have to determine the probabilities and give detailed reasons for my view. Moreover I have heard a much wider range of evidence than would have been admissible in the criminal trial. It will be apparent then, however odd it may seem at first blush, that I could give a different answer to the one given by the jury yet both of us could have correctly answered the questions actually posed to us. Truth is an absolute but elusive concept and the law, in recognising that, deals with it in terms of what can be proved. The fact that something cannot be proved does not mean it did not happen but only that it cannot be proved to the requisite standard that it did. That is the price society has to pay for human fallibility in the quest for truth.

Care proceedings: A special case

Is there ever a winner?

Although a social worker would not start proceedings unless absolutely convinced that the child needed protection, there is often a sense of failure that things have reached that stage at all, as everyone will have worked long and hard to keep the child with the family. When the local authority gets the order it seeks there may be a sense of satisfaction, but never triumph, as there usually is for the victor in other types of court proceedings.

6   *A Local Authority v S, W & T (by his Guardian)* [2004] 2FLR 129, High Court Family Division, p.6–8.

The whole truth

You might think that an applicant would go all out to win, putting his case as strongly as possible and presenting only those selected facts which suit his argument. You would be surprised if you heard someone suing for damages for a car accident volunteering that he himself is a bad driver, was going too fast and the other driver did his best to stop in time. Yet, in care proceedings, the local authority applicant effectively has to do just that. As an arm of the State seeking a Draconian order it has a duty to put the case in a fair and balanced way, pointing out all the facts and considerations which may go against it at the same time as trying to make out its case and secure the order it seeks.

As well as detailing in your evidence all the concerns about the child and family, you therefore also have a duty to point out the parents' love for the child, outline positive aspects of their parenting and acknowledge that your department should have done more to help or should have acted sooner. In this way you provide the court with the proper information to make a decision in the child's best interests.

Multiple parties

Most court cases involve two parties – prosecution and defence, or applicant and respondent. In care proceedings, there are multiple parties. The local authority is the applicant, and the child's mother and the child himself are automatic respondents. The child is always represented by a Children's Guardian (see Chapter 3) and solicitor, but a child who is competent to do so instructs the solicitor himself and the Guardian has to represent herself or find another solicitor. The child's father is a respondent if he has parental responsibility, or if he successfully applies to the court to be made a party. In cases concerning several children, there may also be several fathers, each of whom could be a party and separately represented. Others can apply to be made parties too, if they have a separate case to make, such as grandparents who apply to care for the child. Care proceedings therefore involve a multiplicity of parties, each arguing the case from a different perspective.

Flexible evidential rules

Because care proceedings focus on the child's welfare, the court rules allow greater flexibility of evidence than for other categories of case. Whereas in criminal trials defence lawyers argue every technicality and plead every point, in care cases such tactics do not impress. The combative advocacy in the Crown Court might sway the jury but the care court would frown on the same techniques, demanding a less adversarial approach.

Privacy

In the care court, at present at least, the child is protected by the confidentiality of proceedings. At the time of writing, hearings are not open to anyone other than the parties directly involved, subject to consultation on proposals to allow more public and media access.[7] In the meantime, family judges have shown concern to ensure that media reporting is accurate and balanced. Wall LJ has suggested[8] that in controversial cases judges should prepare a short written summary of their conclusions and reasons to be made publicly available when judgment is delivered. The case in question had received media attention which wrongly implied that the children had been removed because of the parents' learning difficulties. There are also limits on what information arising from proceedings can be disclosed to non-parties without court permission, although since amendments to the Family Proceedings Rules 1991 which came into force on 31 October 2005, restrictions have been considerably relaxed from the former near-absolute prohibition.[9] It is still, however, wise to take legal advice before giving any information to anyone not directly involved in court.

Continuing relationships

In most court cases, the parties never have to see each other again after the trial is over. When care proceedings are finished, the judge, lawyers and Guardian all go away, leaving the social worker to carry on working with the child and family in the aftermath of the court's decision. This has important implications for the way you work with the family before the proceedings and how the case is presented. In general, workers who are honest and clear with families throughout fare much better than those who tread too softly and do not confront issues as they arise. Families can feel betrayed by a worker they thought was 'on their side' who then stands in court spelling out their failings in graphic detail. Equally, some sensitivity is required and being frank about problems does not mean they have to be cruelly expressed – remember you have to carry on after the court proceedings are over.

7   Department for Constitutional Affairs (2006) *Confidence and Confidentiality: Improving Transparency and Privacy in Family Courts* (CP 11/06). London: Department for Constitutional Affairs. Accessed on 1/5/07 at http://www.dca.gov.uk/consult/courttransparencey1106/consultation1106.pdf.

8   *Re H (Freeing Orders: Publicity)* [2006] 1FLR 815; [2005] EWCA Civ 1325, Court of Appeal.

9   Inserted by SI 2005/1976 amended by SI 2005/2922.

Chapter 3

Who's Who

Parties to the proceedings

Party status is an important concept. Only the parties to the proceedings have the automatic right to receive all the papers, to attend all the hearings, to be represented by a lawyer and to put their case by presenting evidence, challenging evidence submitted by others and making legal submissions to the court. Court rules prescribe who is a party depending on the type of case. In care proceedings, the automatic parties are the local authority (applicant), parents with parental responsibility and the child (respondents).

The local authority's lawyer

The relationship between the social worker and the local authority's legal adviser (whether an in-house legal team or a contracted-out private firm) is crucial. Social workers and lawyers are professionals from different fields who should bring their particular skills to the same problem in a spirit of mutual trust, confidence and respect, working as a team to the same end. There should be constructive criticism on both sides – far better to have tough questions and challenges posed by someone on your side when you still have time to work out the answers than to be surprised by the opposing party raising matters which should have been dealt with before.

Remember that your lawyer is just that – a lawyer, not a social worker, and has a different set of competences and skills from you. Legal training is academic, intellectual and analytical. Words are the tools of the lawyer's trade, and lawyers tend to be precise, even pedantic. If your lawyer is experienced in child care work, he may have acquired some knowledge of Social Services matters along the way, but he still does not have your expertise, nor will he ever know the particular child or family. He depends on your 'hands on' work with the family, the factual evidence you provide and the professional skill you apply in interpreting the situation.

Expect to be challenged by your lawyer. He should ask you to explain your actions and why, for example, you provided one service rather than another. He should expect you to explain your views and justify your recommendations. He should point out weaknesses and problems to you and tell you where others will attack. Sometimes this feels dispiriting; you might even feel as if he is not on your side. Far from it – in fact, you should be more concerned if your lawyer accepts everything uncritically you say because you can be sure that the other parties won't!

However, don't be in awe of your lawyer. Feel free to ask questions, request explanations and to put forward your own ideas and suggestions.

The lawyer's job is to advise you on the law and legal procedure, together with the strategy and tactics for presenting the case. He applies the statutory provisions in the Children Act 1989, Human Rights Act 1998, other relevant legislation and case law to the factual information and professional judgments you give him. Make sure you give him all the relevant information, and give it to him straight. Never try to put a favourable gloss on things, skirt around potential problems or miss out difficult issues – he will not thank you if something later comes to light for which he has had no time to prepare. Your communications with him are like a confessional thanks to 'legal professional privilege' – no one else (not even the Children's Guardian) is ever entitled to know what is discussed between solicitor and client or what advice the solicitor gives.

Do you have to follow your lawyer's advice? To the eternal frustration of lawyers, the answer is 'no'. No client is ever bound to take their lawyer's advice, however forcefully given. The lawyer advises, but the client instructs. Lawyers often find themselves having to argue as convincingly and energetically as possible a case or a point they advised their clients not to touch.

Whatever the lawyer's advice, the decision whether or not to commence care proceedings is a matter for the local authority, no one else, not other agencies nor any individual social worker. The local authority is the client and instructs the legal adviser; it is a solicitor/client relationship just like any other. If differences arise between you and the lawyers, remember that you are just the client's representative, not the client yourself, so you must take matters up the line of seniority within your department to resolve the problem, following your authority's procedures for such cases.

One rare exception to the solicitor's obligation to follow a client's instructions is when those instructions conflict with the duty which all lawyers have to the court. A solicitor could not, for example, agree to suppress a piece of evidence which might exonerate the parents, or put forward to the court as true information he knows to be false. He cannot breach your client confidentiality by telling the other parties or the court of your intended deception, but ethically cannot continue to act for you on that basis.

How involved should your lawyer be in case preparation? The reality is that this is usually largely dictated by limited resources. However, investment at the earliest stages – even before the decision to commence proceedings – often pays dividends later on. Poor case preparation can result in a long contested hearing, costing a fortune in legal fees, so skimping on input earlier on is a false economy. Similarly, a face to face meeting with your lawyer may seem like a luxury, but a properly focused discussion can save dozens of memos or emails and make the whole case run more smoothly. The nature and complexity of the case together with the level of experience of the professionals involved determine the best way forward, but always consider holding legal planning meetings before starting proceedings and before any contested hearing.

If you do not feel you are getting the advice and support you need, say so and ask for help. Particularly when you are inexperienced in court work, it is unreasonable for your authority to expect you to work unsupported. We should never forget that these proceedings could determine a child's whole future; they deserve proper preparation.

The authority's lawyers should always be involved in preparing the evidence submitted in support of the case. As a social worker, you should write your own statement, but it should always be closely checked by the lawyer before it is finalised and distributed. In some authorities senior social workers rather than lawyers are supposed to check statements. However senior they may be, their training, experience and perspective is different and with the best will in the world they cannot do a lawyer's job. Any self-respecting lawyer should be extremely unhappy about having to present a case in which he had no input in the preparation of the key evidence. The High Court was clear in the case of *Re R*[1] that statements should be prepared by someone with proper understanding of relevant legal principles, issues in the case and court procedures who should examine all background materials and files and consider what further information or material should be obtained. In that case, a 13-day court hearing took place before evidence came to light forcing the local authority to drop allegations of sexual abuse. Quite apart from the stress that must have caused to all involved, imagine how much money was wasted!

Often you will find that the person you liaise with throughout the preparatory stages does not present the case in court; instead the hearing is handled by a specialist advocate, often a barrister. There can be many reasons for this. Perhaps your legal adviser feels he has insufficient expertise in advocacy, which is a different skill from case preparation; there are specific features of the case that require a specialist or he may simply not be able to spare several days in court and out of the office.

The choice of the right advocate for the case is an important one. Naturally, he should specialise in care proceedings, but beyond that, factors include the

---

1   *Re R (Care: disclosure: nature of proceedings)* [2002] 1FLR 755, High Court Family Division.

level of experience to match the complexity of the case, previous involvement in similar cases and even personality – does the case require a forthright or a subtle approach; passion or a cool head?

You should have a say in choosing the person to present the case in court – after all, it concerns the child, your client. You need to have complete confidence in your advocate. If you do not know the advocate suggested, ask your lawyer why he thinks he is the right choice, and look him up on the internet – most counsels' chambers have a website. Ask your colleagues if they have come across him before. Social Services need to be proactive in sharing information within the department. Every time a social worker goes to court and sees an advocate in action – no matter which party he represents – she should make a note of her impressions and share it with colleagues. There is nothing better than ensuring that someone who gave you a good run for your money in one case is on your side next time! Equally, if an advocate is not impressive, you do not want to entrust your next case to him.

If a barrister or other advocate is to be used for the final hearing, he should be instructed early on. Short of a genuine emergency, there is no excuse for last minute instructions. If you are the key worker in a case, you should have a meeting with the barrister – known as a 'conference with counsel' – well before the hearing. This gives you a chance to discuss the case in detail and for you to get to know each other before the big day.

Build in time for proper feedback and reflection with your legal team at the end of the case. Too often the response when the hearing is over is to breathe a sigh of relief and rush on to the next case, so we fail to learn lessons and are forced to re-invent the wheel or repeat mistakes time and again. Every case should teach us something, and that learning needs to be shared with the whole department – otherwise one team could learn an important lesson only to have someone from another team repeat the same mistake, possibly in front of the same judge, the following week.

QUESTIONS FOR REFLECTION

- What can you do to make your relationship with your lawyers work?
- Could any inter-departmental procedures be introduced to improve teamwork with lawyers?

The parents

You are a professional, working as part of a team and supported by colleagues from your own and other departments. For you, the case is part of the job you have chosen to do. The case is not about you; it is not personal. For the parents, it is a different story – the case could not be more personal; their life histories are examined, the most intimate aspects of their lives dissected and, at the end of it all, they may lose their children.

For a moment put aside your professional conviction that what you are doing is the right thing for the child and put yourself in the parents' position. How would you feel in their shoes? How would you behave? Of course, circumstances of care cases vary widely and parents come from differing backgrounds with a range of difficulties, but almost invariably they love their children and believe that they are in the right, that you are wrong and your action is unjustified. This dictates their response to proceedings. Remembering this will help you to keep a cool head when you are faced with a response you think is unreasonable, unfair or even aggressive.

Use your knowledge of the particular parents in your case to anticipate how they are likely to react and what they are likely to say and do. Discuss these anticipated responses with your legal team and prepare in advance how to deal with them.

Occasionally a parent involved in proceedings is incapable of understanding the proceedings and giving instructions to a solicitor because of profound learning disability or severe mental health problems. In those circumstances, the parent's interests may be represented by the Official Solicitor (commonly known as the OS), a central government appointee with an office staffed by civil servants. Only the County or High Court can invite the OS to act, and he requires medical or psychiatric confirmation of the parent's condition before consenting to take on the case. The OS then appoints a solicitor, gives instructions on the parent's behalf and files a report in the proceedings. The role is strictly limited to representing adults while they are incapacitated so if, for example, the mother's mental health improves during the proceedings, the OS withdraws and the mother can instruct her own solicitor.

The parent's legal representative

All parents in care proceedings are entitled to have competent representation from a solicitor who specialises in care proceedings. Although you might be tempted to think that your life might be easier if the parents were not well represented, in fact cases go much more smoothly if everyone involved is competent. As a matter of principle, no one should have a child removed without having their case properly argued and the child himself needs to know that his parents were fairly treated by the system.

The parent's solicitor has a challenging job. He has to go through the evidence in detail with his clients, ensuring they understand it and noting their responses. Where clients have learning difficulties, mental health or personality problems, cannot read or are simply and understandably emotional, this is a lengthy and delicate task. Just because the solicitor is 'on their side' does not mean that he is immune from parents' sometimes angry or emotional responses

– parents' solicitors can be on the receiving end of verbal abuse, insults or threats from difficult or distressed clients. Except in cases extreme enough to justify the solicitor refusing to continue to act, this is all part of the job, and the solicitor should not let anyone else know that the working relationship is anything other than harmonious.

The solicitor's job is to advise his client on the law and the strength of the evidence, on the response to the allegations, legal procedures, strategies and tactics. Sometimes this includes telling the parents that the local authority's case is so strong that, no matter what, they are likely to lose their children. The parents may accept that, and the strategy then turns to damage limitation, such as accepting a care order, but seeking more contact. On the other hand they may insist on fighting the case come what may. If so, the solicitor must follow his instructions and find a way of putting up a convincing fight, however futile he knows it to be. You will never know that, in private, the solicitor has told his clients their case is hopeless. Do not assume that a lawyer actually believes in the case he is presenting, however passionately he appears to do so!

Sometimes a parent has to fight on two fronts. For example, two parents may each blame the other for injuries to the child. For each, the objective is two-fold – first, to defeat Social Services' criticisms and second, to lay the blame on the other parent.

The Children's Guardian and the child's solicitor

The role of Children's Guardian, formerly known as the Guardian ad Litem, was developed after the scandal of Maria Colwell's death. Maria died in 1973, aged seven, at the hands of her stepfather, after she had been returned from the safety of foster care with the agreement of the Local Authority, court and her mother. The enquiry into her death highlighted the need for an independent voice for the child in proceedings. The Children Act 1975 made fundamental changes to the child protection system, including the creation of the Guardian ad Litem's role.

The child is always a party to care proceedings, and increasingly this is also the case in private law Children Act proceedings. The Guardian is the professional who represents the child's interests, but as a party, the child is also entitled to legal representation. His solicitor, a member of the Law Society's Children Panel, must do the work on the case personally wherever possible. If the child is too young to give his own instructions, the solicitor and Guardian work together, the Guardian effectively acting as the client, giving instructions to the solicitor, who in turn advises the Guardian on law, evidence, procedure, strategy and tactics. The working relationship should be robust, mutually respectful and challenging and, as with all solicitor/client relationships, discussions between the two are confidential.

If the child is competent to do so, he gives his own instructions to the solicitor. If these conflict with the Guardian's views the child's solicitor and the Guardian end up putting forward different cases to the court.

The question of a child's competence to instruct is one for the solicitor concerned. Age is one factor; the older the child, the more likely he is to be competent and the issue is at least considered for any child of secondary school age. The child's level of understanding is also relevant and learning difficulties or emotional problems can impede competence to instruct. Even where a child instructs the solicitor himself, unlike other parties, he is unlikely to file a formal statement, attend court or give evidence.

The child's team's job is to put forward an independent view of the child's best interests and to ensure that his wishes and feelings are made clear to the court. No doubt you feel that you are already doing this – after all, the child is your client too and you are only taking action because you and your department believe it to be the best thing for the child. You may also feel that you know the child and his wishes and feelings better than the Guardian, and you may be right – if so, you can make this point to the court in due course. But the fact is that your authority has, by taking the proceedings in the first place, already nailed its colours to the mast and is inevitably in a partisan position at the very outset of the case. The Guardian and the child's solicitor come in afresh and look at the case with new eyes, testing, challenging and double checking.

Guardians vary enormously in approach and style. They are more autonomous than local authority social workers, not hidebound by departmental procedures. They also tend to be independent personalities – few shrinking violets apply for the post. Some work cases very actively; others take a more hands-off approach. Some give clear indications of their thinking from the start, others play their cards closer to their chests. Some seem to feel the need to assert their independence by apparent hostility to Social Services. However, even if a Guardian works closely with you, remember she is not your supervisor – it is not her role to advise you on how to work your case or to help you through your difficulties, and she should always scrupulously retain her independence.

Always treat the Guardian with respect (the court certainly will), listen to her views and take her comments into account – but do not feel obliged to agree with her or follow her bidding. However authoritative she may be, the Guardian is not the court and does not make the final decision, nor is the court bound to follow her recommendation. If, after proper consideration, you and your department disagree with the Guardian, stick to your guns, and be prepared to justify your position and explain your reasoning.

Guardians are social workers by training, and their qualifications are the same as yours. As with any profession, some are better than others. Many guardians are excellent but some are not. On occasions you may feel that the Guardian has not spent enough time with the child, or has not approached a case with sufficient diligence, objectivity or competence. Children deserve better than that and the local authority should be willing to challenge inadequate work by a Guardian (you can be sure a Guardian will have no hesitation in pointing out any inadequacies on the local authority's part). Your advocate should be instructed, for example, to suggest to the court that your view of the child, formed over a long period of consistent work, should be preferred to that of a Guardian who has seen the child only on a few occasions.

Under s42 Children Act 1989, the Guardian is entitled to examine and take copies of any Social Services records relating to the proceedings or to the child. She can then include those documents or refer to them in her report or her evidence in court. As a matter of courtesy, she should tell you which documents she is copying and what she is proposing to use. She is not entitled to see your legal advice or any correspondence or notes of discussions between you and your lawyers, which are covered by legal professional privilege. If you are in any doubt about what documents the Guardian should see, consult your lawyers.

The case of *Re R* (mentioned above) also makes it clear that Guardians should, like social workers, be more prepared to produce their notes of relevant conversations and incidents. Feel free, therefore, to ask the Guardian to provide a copy of her notes, for example, of an important interview with the child.

QUESTIONS FOR REFLECTION

- What is your attitude towards Guardians in general? How does this affect your working relationships with them?
- How can you achieve the right balance of co-operation and independence when working with Guardians?

The court

The court – judge or magistrates – is entrusted with the job of deciding the case. This sounds obvious, but think for a moment what it actually entails. How would you like to have to decide whether a child should be permanently separated from his parents? Imagine the burden of that responsibility. In that position, what would you want from the parties? When you are preparing and giving your evidence think how it would feel to be in the court's shoes and provide information to help the judge or magistrates perform their difficult task.

Judges are qualified and experienced lawyers, trained to analyse facts against a legal framework. Certain County Court judges are designated to hear public law cases, known in the jargon as having a 'care ticket'. In the High Court, care cases are heard by judges who sit exclusively in the Family Division. Magistrates, on the other hand, have no legal qualifications and sit part-time alongside their other occupations. Care cases are heard by magistrates selected according to aptitude for the Family Panel. Their strengths lie in common sense and life experience.

When you picture a judge in your mind's eye, do you see a man or a woman? Is this person young? Black? Disabled? Openly gay? The fact is that although things are changing, most judges are still male, especially in the higher echelons of the judiciary – Lady Hale became the first woman appointed to the House of Lords as recently as 2004. Minority groups are under-represented – as at 1 April 2007 only one out of the 108 High Court judges came from an ethnic minority. Most judges are former barristers rather than solicitors, and tend to come from a relatively narrow social group. As for age – by definition, judges cannot be young as eligibility even to apply for judicial posts depends on specified periods already spent as qualified lawyers. It then takes time to climb the judicial ladder and so, at the time of writing, half of the judges in the House of Lords are in their seventies, with the other half not far behind. This also means that social changes take time to work through to the upper levels of the judiciary.

Judges are primarily lawyers and although as part of their judicial training they have to cover some other topics, such as equal opportunities, by definition they have a limited range of academic and professional experience.

Magistrates, in contrast, are far more diverse and socially representative. The previous 'twin-set and pearls' image is now outdated thanks to a positive effort to appoint magistrates from varied backgrounds, ethnic groups, social classes and age groups – in September 2006 a 19-year-old woman was appointed as a magistrate. They also represent a wide range of professions (except law and those too closely related to the work of the courts) and life experiences. On the other hand, they do not necessarily have the academic background or intellectual ability of judges, although they undergo a carefully designed programme of training.

QUESTION FOR REFLECTION

- How might the composition of the court affect the way you present your evidence?

Frequently asked questions

What's the difference between a lawyer, advocate, counsel, solicitor and barrister?

Lawyer is a generic term for all legal professionals including solicitors, barristers and academics. *Advocate* is the term for the person who presents the case in court, whichever branch of the legal profession they belong to. *Counsel* is another name for a barrister.

Solicitors and barristers form the two main branches of the legal profession. Their training separates after the degree stage, both then undertaking a combination of further study and practical training. Solicitors work directly with their clients, whereas barristers are briefed by solicitors, who still send papers tied up with red tape. Solicitors deal with correspondence and negotiations and also have the right of audience in some courts including all levels of court in family proceedings but cannot appear in the Crown Court, which is reserved for barristers, who have the right of audience in all courts. Barristers often specialise in advocacy and also give written opinions on complex points of law.

What is a QC and when would one be involved in a case?

QC stands for Queen's Counsel, also often known as a 'silk' (the fabric of their gowns). Only senior members of the profession are eligible to be appointed as QCs and the vast majority are barristers. They are only involved in exceptionally complicated cases and often are not instructed until the case reaches the appeal courts.

What is the Children Panel?

Administered by the Law Society, this consists of specialist solicitors who have attended a training course, demonstrated technical knowledge of family law and practical experience of care cases, attended an interview and provided references.

How can a lawyer represent a paedophile, or someone he knows is guilty?

Dr Johnson summed this up perfectly in the eighteenth century:

> a lawyer has no business with the justice or injustice of the cause which he undertakes, unless the client asks his opinion and then he is bound to give it honestly. The justice or injustice of the cause is to be decided by the judge.

Quite simply the lawyer's job is to be the client's specialist mouthpiece, and every client is entitled to be represented to the best of the lawyer's ability. The lawyer's private view of the case or his client is entirely irrelevant.

Do parties in care proceedings always get Legal Aid?

At the time of writing, in care proceedings, parents and children automatically have the right to receive Legal Aid, regardless of their means or the merits of their case. However, the Legal Aid system is under strain, lawyers are increasingly reluctant to undertake Legal Aid work due to poor remuneration and excessive bureaucracy, and there are constant proposals for reform.

What qualifications do Children's Guardians have?

Children and Family Courts Advisory and Support Service (CAFCASS) require a minimum of a Diploma in Social Work (DipSW) or Certificate of Qualification in Social Work (CQSW) and three years' post-qualification experience in social work practice with children and families.

What is meant by HHJ, J and LJ

These are abbreviations for judge's titles. HHJ Brown refers to a County Court judge, His or Her Honour Judge Brown. A High Court judge is Mr or Mrs Justice Brown, shortened to Brown J. LJ after the judge's name shows that he or she has reached the Court of Appeal, and stands for Lord or Lady Justice.

How do lawyers find reports of decided cases?

There are official law reports for decided cases, such as the All England Law Reports and Weekly Law Reports. There are also specialist reports, the most important of which, for our purposes, is the Family Law Reports. The name of the case in children's matters gives only an initial, rather than a name, to preserve confidentiality and further details give an indication of the case content. The report reference consists of the year of the case in square brackets, then the volume of the reports, report series and page number. Thus, the case referred to in this chapter is *Re R (Care: Disclosure: Nature of Proceedings)* [2002] 1FLR 755, meaning that it can be found in volume 1 of the Family Law Reports for 2002 at page 755.

Chapter 4

Evidence

The idea of evidence

Both parties want to win the case. To persuade the court, each party puts his case to court by a combination of evidence, giving his own version of events, and argument, asking the court to interpret the evidence in his favour.

Academic lawyers write volumes and practising lawyers argue for hours about the law of evidence. This chapter, therefore, can only give an essential outline. Fortunately for social workers, the rules of evidence in care proceedings are more relaxed than in almost any other kind of case.

Put at its most basic, evidence is the information which a court can take into account in making its decision. Rules of 'admissibility of evidence' determine what information the court is allowed to hear; if information is inadmissible, the court cannot even consider it, however relevant or convincing it might seem to be, however much the court might wish to or justice might seem to demand it.

If evidence is admissible, the court can take it into account. It is then up to the court to decide how much weight to give it – that is, to decide how plausible or persuasive it is. It is important, therefore, not to confuse admissibility with weight – just because something is admissible does not mean that it is convincing, or adds anything to the case. Not all admissible evidence is worth presenting to the court.

Think of the classic image of the scales of justice – two scale pans suspended in balance. Each party puts his evidence onto his side of the scales in an effort to make them tip his way. Only admissible evidence can be put into the scales, but the mere fact that something is allowed does not mean it will have any effect – you can put a feather onto the scales, but it will not make the scales move.

Burden of proof

The concept of the 'burden of proof' essentially determines whose job it is to make the scales move his way, and the general principle of English law is that it is up to the party bringing the case to prove it. So, in a criminal case, the prosecution must prove that the defendant committed the crime; it is not up to the defendant to show that he is innocent. In care proceedings, it is the local authority's job to prove that the threshold criteria are met and the child's welfare demands the making of an order; the parents do not have to prove that they are 'good enough'.

In court, the applicant (the prosecution in a criminal trial, the local authority in care proceedings) presents its case first and attempts to prove it by putting its evidence into the scales, making them move in its favour. The defendant/respondent cross-examines the applicant's witnesses to undermine the impact of the evidence, so that although the information may still be in the final reckoning, its weight reduced.

That defendant/respondent in turn produces his own case, to undermine or neutralise the applicant's evidence – effectively to remove weight from the applicant's side of the scales – and to put evidence into his own scale pan to tip the balance in his favour.

Standard of proof

The next question is how far the scales have to move to allow the applicant to 'win'. This is the basic concept of the 'standard of proof', discussed in Chapter 2. In a criminal case, to achieve proof beyond reasonable doubt, the prosecution have to tip the scales much further than the applicant in a civil matter.

Is the standard always the same?

It is very important not to be complacent and think that the civil standard is an easy hurdle to overcome. This is particularly so when your allegations are serious. In the case of *Re H and R*[1] the House of Lords considered what the civil standard actually means. The case concerned two younger half-sisters of a girl who alleged sexual abuse by her stepfather, the father of the younger two. There were no concerns for the two girls other than the older girl's allegations. Logically, therefore, they were only at risk of significant harm if the older girl had been sexually abused, so the case turned on whether the local authority could establish her allegations were true on the balance of probabilities.

In the event, although considerable suspicions were aroused, the evidence was not strong enough to prove the allegations. As Lord Nicholls said, 'a conclusion that the child is suffering or is likely to suffer significant harm must be based on facts, not just suspicion' (p.102C), and 'an alleged but non-proven

---

1   *Re H & R (Child sexual abuse: Standard of proof)* [1996] 1 FLR 80, House of Lords, p.101 G–H.

fact is not a fact'(p.99H). Likelihood of harm to the younger girls was not established, and the threshold criteria were not made out.

Considering the standard of proof, Lord Nicholls said:

> The balance of probability standard means that a court is satisfied an event occurred if the court considers that, on the evidence, the occurrence of the event was more likely than not. When assessing the probabilities the court will have in mind as a factor, to whatever extent is appropriate in the particular case, that the more serious the allegation the less likely it is that the event occurred and, hence, the stronger should be the evidence before the court concludes that the allegation is established on the balance of probability…
> Built into the preponderance of probability standard is a generous degree of flexibility in respect of the seriousness of the allegation…the inherent probability or improbability of an event is itself a matter to be taken into account when weighing the probabilities and deciding whether, on balance, an event occurred. The more improbable the event, the stronger must be the evidence that it did occur before, on the balance of probability, its occurrence will be established. (p.96B – E)

Lord Nicholls was anxious to stress that this did not mean that he had changed the standard of proof – the balance of probabilities still applies. However, to continue the scales analogy, it is as if the mechanism is stiffer so that greater force is required to move the scales the same distance.

To illustrate this in simple terms, imagine two allegations made against a social worker:

1. She made personal use of the office photocopier without authorisation.

2. She embezzled £250,000 from the department.

Which of the two allegations are you more likely to believe? How much evidence would you require to satisfy you that the first allegation was true? Would the same amount of evidence satisfy you of the second allegation? Most people have little difficulty believing the first allegation. The second allegation, on the other hand, seems inherently improbable and demands hard evidence to make it credible. Lord Nicholls's reasoning is, essentially, no more than that.

Two practical problems arise from this case. First, just because some things happen infrequently does not mean that they do not happen at all; some people do embezzle huge sums from their employers, and some stepfathers do sexually abuse their stepdaughters. It is arguable that few 16-year-olds make allegations of sexual abuse, so the fact that the allegation was made at all already took the case outside the realm of the inherently probable.

Second, one effect of Re H and R is that it means that the more serious the risk to the child and the more grave the consequences of not protecting him, then the harder it is to prove the case. You may find this counter-intuitive.

However, their Lordships' decision is the authoritative statement of the law, so we have no choice but to work within it. It is worth considering the practical implications for your cases.

If you make a serious allegation, you have to have the hard evidence to prove it. You cannot afford to be casual about it, or rely on the court drawing the same inferences as you. If your case is any way unusual or something which the court may instinctively find difficult to believe, you and your lawyers need to pay particular attention to finding evidence to establish every single aspect of the case.

Scenarios in the 'inherently improbable' category might include:

- ritual or organised abuse
- sexual abuse by female perpetrators
- sexual abuse of young infants
- abuse of children with disabilities
- allegations against pillars of the community
- factitious/induced illness.

The list could go on, and no doubt you can think of other categories to add.

In such cases you need to really pin down your evidence. Suspicions and gut feelings will not suffice, but there may be evidence underlying those feelings. If you analyse it, there is a reason behind your instinctive reactions – why do you feel as you do? 'He gives me the creeps' is not evidence; 'he frequently turns the conversation to sexual topics' or 'he avoids eye contact whenever the subject of sexual abuse is raised' are at least factual observations and might well be evidence when seen in context.

Lord Nicholls himself observed in *Re H and R* that evidence may include matters which in themselves seem minor or even trivial, but become significant when seen in context. Think of a jigsaw: each piece on its own is meaningless – it is only when all the pieces are put together that the picture emerges. When you are building a case you need to make sure that you give the court all the pieces of the jigsaw.

QUESTION FOR REFLECTION

- What are the implications of *Re H and R* for your practice?

Types of evidence

Factual evidence

Clearly, the most fundamental form of evidence is plain factual information which tells the court 'this is what happened', 'this is what I did' or 'this is what I saw'. It comes from eye witnesses, and people directly involved in events. Whether the person is telling the truth or not is a matter for the court to judge.

Real and documentary evidence

The court is not limited to considering words; objects can be evidence, the classic example being exhibiting the alleged murder weapon in a criminal court. This is less common in family cases, but occasionally objects are produced, such as the belt used to hit a child.

Documents can be relevant, including photographs. Police photos or video recordings of a drugs raid, for example, can be powerful evidence, showing exactly what home conditions were like. Photographs of a child's injuries can be vitally important, remembering of course that injuries such as bruises must be photographed quickly before they fade. In one case where the child had almost died from malnutrition, photographs taken on his admission to hospital were produced alongside photographs taken after three months in foster care. He was transformed from a bag of bones to a normal healthy-looking child. The pictures were worth a thousand words.

Diagrams or graphs can also be valuable evidence. In care proceedings, centile charts are often produced by health professionals, and these can be graphic in both senses. One chart showed a child's growth as flat, falling further and further away from the original centile, until a particular date when it suddenly shot up steeply, recording remarkable catch-up growth. The rest of the evidence demonstrated that the dramatic change coincided with the date the father left home. In other cases, you may find a similar change after reception into foster care. A simple line on a chart can speak volumes.

Video recordings can also be produced in evidence and are especially important for interviews with children. If these are conducted following the 'Achieving Best Evidence'[2] guidelines, they can be produced in both criminal and care cases. Interviewing children is a skilled task, and should only be undertaken by specially trained and experienced staff. Properly done, video interviews can be powerful. They have the advantage of recording not only the

2   Home Office Communication Directorate (2002) *Achieving Best Evidence in Criminal Proceedings: Guidance for Vulnerable or Intimidated Witnesses, Including Children.* London: Home Office. Accessed on 1/5/07 at http://www.homeoffice.gov.uk/documents/achieving-best-evidence/.

child's responses, but also the questions asked, so the court and parties can clearly see whether the child has in any way been led by the questioner. As well as hearing the child's words, viewers can see his body language. In one interview a bright, cheery five-year-old physically crumpled as soon as the subject of sexual abuse was raised. There was no substitute for seeing the video – paragraphs of description would never have conveyed what the viewers saw. In another case the interview transcript showed that the child said 'Daddy hurt my bottom', and those who believed that he had been sexually abused could easily have leapt to the conclusion that this was a disclosure. In fact, the video revealed that, as he said these words, the child clearly gestured with his hand in a smacking motion – he was telling us that his father spanked him.

Whenever real or photographic evidence is produced, it must be authenticated, for example, by the person who took the photograph, confirming that this is indeed the photograph he took, when, where and how it was done and confirming that it accurately records what he saw. The other parties must be sent copies of such evidence in advance, as well as transcripts of audio or video recordings.

QUESTION FOR REFLECTION

• What information other than written evidence can you use to establish your case?

Hearsay evidence

Put simply, hearsay evidence is anything which is not from the witness's own direct experience. The starting point of English law was always that hearsay was inadmissible, for the simple reason that it is generally of no use to the court. Imagine a witness telling a criminal court that he heard that the defendant had robbed the bank. What use would that be? All the witness could confirm was that he heard it, and give details about who told him, where, when, how – but he could not tell the court one way or the other whether it was true. He would waste the court's time.

Hearsay does not just refer to information heard, but really anything other than evidence from the witness's own direct experience. This includes reports from other professionals ('the health visitor told me the home was unhygienic'), or information from the file prior to your involvement ('my predecessor discussed hygiene with Mrs X').

What children tell you is hearsay evidence. In Scenario 2.1 (Chapter 2), Amy's allegations of sexual abuse against her stepfather Barry are recorded in a video interview. At Barry's criminal trial, the video is shown to the Crown Court, but it cannot stand alone; someone has to be cross-examined to test out her evidence. The interviewers cannot give evidence for Amy – that would be hearsay. The only person who can give Amy's evidence in the criminal court is Amy herself. Thanks to the provisions of the Youth Justice and Criminal Evidence Act 1999, some concessions are made to Amy – for example, she gives evidence by live TV link rather than in the courtroom itself, and the barristers and judge remove their wigs and gowns, but the fact remains that Amy herself has to go to court to answer questions.

Amy is also subject to care proceedings. Because of an important exception for children's cases (the Children (Admissibility of Hearsay Evidence) Order 1993) this time Amy does not have to go to court. Her video is shown to the court, and the interviewers can give evidence about what she said. The hearsay evidence itself is admissible.

Box 4.1: Children (Admissibility of Hearsay Evidence) Order 1993

In –

    (a)   civil proceedings before the High Court or a County Court; and

    (b)   (i)   family proceedings, and

             (ii) civil proceedings, under the Child Support Act 1991 in a magistrates' court,

evidence given in connection with the upbringing, maintenance or welfare of a child shall be admissible notwithstanding any rule of law relating to hearsay (Clause 2, SI 1993 No. 621).[3]

This exception does not just apply to formal interviews: foster carers, teachers and social workers can tell the court what the child said and the court can take this information fully into account. Sometimes applications are made to the court to insist on the child coming to court despite these provisions, using the arguments of the right to a fair trial and the need for direct, rather than hearsay, evidence. Such applications succeed only in the most exceptional circumstances. On 19 January 2007 the Court of Appeal considered the case of a 10-year-old girl known as 'L'[4]. The judgments emphasise that it is undesirable for a child to have to give evidence in care proceedings and that particular

---

3   Office of Public Sector Information (1993) *Children (Admissibility of Hearsay Evidence) Order.* London: OPSI. Accessed on 1/5/2007 at http://www.opsi.gov.uk/SI/si199306.htm.

4   *LM (a child by her Guardian) v Medway Council and RM and YM* [2007] EWCA Civ 9.

justification is needed before a court should issue a witness summons against a child. However, this was one such exceptional case. The key difficulty in the case was that the first person to make allegations against L's father was not L herself but her mother. L then made essentially the same allegations in interview. By the time of the final care hearing, the mother was not only saying that the allegations were untrue, but she had coached L into making them. No one knew what L would say without hearing from her in person. The Court of Appeal held that in this case, the judge's need to hear L's own evidence outweighed the possible psychological harm giving evidence might cause her. Wilson LJ was, however, at pains to stress that this situation was:

> quite different from that...which obtains in the vast majority of public law applications. The present case does not reflect the straightforward situation in which a parent who has been accused by a child denies the accusation and aspires to cross-examine her or him. (paragraph [61])

This case should not, therefore, be used as a precedent to summons children to court in anything but the most unusual circumstances.

The hearsay exception is not limited to evidence from children themselves but can apply to information from anyone in a children's case. Sometimes social workers' statements seem to be nothing but hearsay, reporting information from the police, health visitor, teacher and family care worker. It may be admissible, but is it helpful to the court? Is it the best way of presenting the information?

Scenario 4.1: Hearsay or direct evidence

Mrs Goff, health visitor, makes a referral to Ms Hutchinson, social worker about baby Ian. There are two ways of giving this information to court:

1. Ms Hutchinson can record in her statement: 'Mrs Goff the health visitor telephoned me to report her concerns that Ian was being handled roughly by his mother.' This gives the court the basic facts, but what can be tested about this statement? Ms Hutchinson can be asked whether the conversation really happened, and the exact words Mrs Goff used, but can she give any more information to the court? The answers to any further questions – what Mrs Goff saw, why she was concerned, what she did about it, how experienced she is – must be 'I'm sorry, you'd have to ask Mrs Goff about that.'

> 2.   Mrs Goff can make her own statement to the court and, if
>   required, attend to give oral evidence. She can set out her
>   qualifications and experience and describe exactly what she
>   saw and what she did about it. Her evidence can be tested
>   out by cross-examination, giving the court the opportunity
>   to form a view about her reliability and professionalism. Her
>   first-hand evidence is bound to be more vivid and detailed
>   than anything Ms Hutchinson could report. Ms Hutchinson
>   can refer to Mrs Goff's evidence briefly in her own state-
>   ment when she pulls together all the concerns for Ian.
>
> If you were the judge, which would you prefer?

Should adults who make allegations have the same protection as children? Imagine the case of a couple applying to look after their granddaughter who needs a home. Sixteen years ago, they fostered a girl, now adult, who for the first time alleges that the husband sexually abused her when she was in the couple's care. The social worker interviews the woman, believes her and reports on her interview in evidence to the FPC. Is that good enough?

That was the scenario in the case Re D[5] The FPC made a finding on the basis of the social worker's hearsay evidence that the allegation was true. The grandparents appealed and won – the magistrates had no right to accept evidence in that form or to make a finding. The President of the Family Division of the High Court declared her dismay at the 'sloppy half-hearted…sympathetic interview without any sort of rigour of questioning…to have that accepted by the court as evidence that brands a man as a sexual abuser is entirely unacceptable'. Essentially, children may be protected from coming to the family court, but adults are expected to stand up for themselves.

Notice the consequences of the inadequate work in this case. If the grandfather was innocent, he and his family suffered the stress of false allegations and the child's placement was delayed. If the allegations were true, the inadequacy of the case presentation placed the granddaughter at risk.

The general principle is that the court is always entitled to the best evidence available – that is, direct personal evidence wherever possible. You owe it to the court and to the child to present the case as strongly as possible.

5   Re D *(Sexual abuse allegations: evidence of adult victim)* [2002] 1FLR 723, High Court Family Division, p.728D.

Whenever you are preparing a case, consider who should give evidence about each point you need to prove. Your lawyer does not know who is involved in a child's life unless you tell him, and so he does not know who to approach for evidence without your assistance. As part of your case preparation you and your legal team need to consider who can provide all the pieces of the jigsaw.

If hearsay is unavoidable, explain the reason why direct evidence is not available, for example, that the original social worker has emigrated to Australia, or that the lay informant asked to remain anonymous.

Remember, too, that just because you are the key worker representing your department, that does not mean that you have to give every piece of social work evidence yourself. For example, if your care plan for the child is adoption, the court needs evidence about how realistic the plan is and how quickly adopters can be found. If you are not an adoption specialist, you may not have the relevant information or experience, so a member of the adoption team needs to give that evidence.

Similarly, if a decision in the case was made by a senior member of your department, then only she can explain why that decision was reached and she needs to be prepared to come to court. If another worker tries to explain a decision which was not hers, she is giving the court second-hand evidence.

Nor can you answer for other agencies or departments within your authority. For example, if a child has received inadequate educational provision, it is for an education representative, not you, to explain it. Sometimes just a letter from the legal department requesting evidence or court attendance works wonders in securing services!

If the authority is likely to be criticised, or there is an issue about broader policy, it is wrong for a career grade social worker to take the flak – a senior member of the department should attend. This did not happen in the case of *Re F: F v Lambeth LBC*[6] where the poor inexperienced social worker was left on her own to explain to the High Court why no adequate care plan had been provided for two boys who had been in Lambeth's care for ten years. As the judge put it:

> I was treated to the scarcely edifying spectacle of this hapless Ms H being cross-examined in default of anyone else produced on behalf of Lambeth both by the parents' counsel and by the Official Solicitor's counsel…on matters for which she bore absolutely no personal responsibility and which, it seems to me, required explanation and justification by figures very much more senior and, if she will forgive me for saying so, more experienced than Ms H.

6   Re F: F v Lambeth LBC [2002] 1FLR 217, High Court Family Division, p.223 [16].

The judge paid tribute to Ms H's professional integrity and moral courage, but senior managers should have been there to carry the can. Why no one sought a witness summons to require a senior officer to come to court is a mystery. There is no reason why any career grade social worker should be in that position and senior managers should take the responsibility which is rightfully theirs.

Opinion evidence

What is an opinion? Sometimes it is explicit, for example, 'in my professional opinion she is suffering from postnatal depression'. However, consider sentences like 'John shows disturbed behaviour' or 'Mr Kent was drunk when he came to the meeting'. These are expressed as if they are facts, but what is or is not 'disturbed' is a value judgement – an opinion – and it is doubtful that you performed a breathalyser test on Mr Kent to establish his alcohol consumption; your observations of his behaviour and demeanour led you to the opinion that he was drunk. Be clear in your own mind whether you are actually reporting facts or expressing an opinion.

The starting point of English law is that opinion evidence is generally inadmissible, because most of the time it is useless. Any witness could express a view about whether or not the child should go home but how would that help the court? In most cases, it is simply a waste of the court's time, and anyway, the question of whether the child goes home is the court's job. The only time a witness's opinion is worth considering is when it is based on expertise which the court itself does not have. For that reason, there is an exception to the general rule, allowing experts to give opinion evidence if, but only if, it is relevant and necessary. Cazalet J in *Re R*[7] said:

> expert witnesses are in a privileged position; indeed only experts are permitted to give an opinion in evidence. Outside the legal field the court itself has no expertise and for that reason frequently has to rely on the evidence of experts.

Experts

Who, then, is an expert? How can expertise be established? Ultimately it is for the court to decide whether a particular witness is an expert and, if there is a dispute, there can be a mini trial within a trial for the court to determine the issue. Expertise can be established by formal qualifications and training but also by experience. For example, a foster mother without a piece of paper to her

---

7   *Re R (A minor) (Expert evidence)* [1991] 1FLR 291, High Court Family Division, p.292C.

name but who has fostered 50 pre-adopt babies has expertise and can assist the court with her opinions on the care and behaviour of young babies. Conversely, a witness who happens to have a psychology degree acquired ten years ago, but who has never practised in the field is unlikely to be able to help the court on psychological issues.

QUESTION FOR REFLECTION

• Are you an expert? If so, what are you an expert in?

One common feature of social workers as professionals is a remarkable lack of confidence in their own expertise. Ask a room full of doctors or lawyers if they are experts and you will be there all day while they expound on the breadth and profundity of their skill. Ask the same question to a room full of social workers and the response is usually silence, followed by some apologetic mumblings and comments about being a jack of all trades but master of none. Social workers at times seem almost to conspire in the de-skilling of their own profession.

If you really have no expertise then you have no right to offer your opinions or recommendations to the court – you can only stick to the facts. If this is the case, then how can you bring care proceedings which by definition require you to have formed a professional opinion that the child needs protection?

The fact is that social workers do have expertise. You have qualifications and experience (which may include relevant previous professional experience or activities in a private capacity, such as being a youth leader).

Take time to consider what you do know and what expertise you have to assist the court. If you are challenged in court on what right you have to reach a particular recommendation, you need to know how to justify your status as an expert – you will hardly look a credible professional if you cannot answer!

It is equally important to know where your boundaries lie, and where are the limits of your expertise. One of the problems of social work is that it is a broad subject; for example, you know about child development, but not as much as a paediatrician; you know about family functioning, but not as much as a psychologist. Be very careful never to get drawn in beyond the limits of your knowledge or seem to be claiming expertise you do not have, or you will find yourself in difficulties – but don't be afraid to claim the knowledge you do have.

Generally it is best to avoid telling the court who or what to believe – that is the court's job and it needs no help on that score. Occasionally the court may need assistance in understanding a child's testimony, such as explaining the nuances of a child's body language on video or interpreting his behaviour, and this may extend to advising the court on the child's credibility, but it must truly be expert evidence and not simply an account of who or what you believe.

Opinions and conclusions must always be based on the factual evidence to which the expert has applied his learning and experience. Facts and opinions should therefore be closely intertwined and it should be clear how one flows from the other. Sometimes the facts speak so clearly for themselves that the opinion scarcely needs to be expressed at all; as Lawton LJ said in *R v Turner*[8] 'If on the proven facts a judge or jury can form their own conclusions without help, then the opinion of an expert is unnecessary.'

As a professional working with the child and family, you have a dual role. You provide some of the core factual evidence on which the whole case is based, and you also offer opinions and recommendations which flow from your own observations. If you are the key worker, you also take into account the information you have received from others.

Some expert witnesses are called into a case just for the purpose of an opinion for the proceedings – they have no other involvement with the child or family. Although such experts inevitably also provide some factual evidence (for example, a psychiatrist outlines the details of his examination of the mother and what she said to him) the court's primary focus is on the expert's opinion.

Anyone claiming expertise and expressing opinions to the court has a duty to the court. This was explained by Cazalet J in the case of *Re R* cited above:

> ... experts must express only opinions which they genuinely hold and which are not biased in favour of one particular party...
>
> The expert should not mislead by omissions. He should consider all the material facts in reaching his conclusions, and must not omit to consider the material facts which could detract from his concluded opinion. (p.292C)

Your duty is to be balanced and objective, despite the fact that you are arguing for a particular outcome. You cannot pick only the facts which suit your conclusion and conveniently ignore the rest.

At the end of the case, the expert evidence is weighed in the balance by the court along with all of the other information in the case. The judge or magistrates are in no way bound to follow the expert's view; as Ward LJ said in *Re B*[9] 'the expert advises, but the judge decides'.

8   *R v Turner* [1975] QB 834, Court of Appeal, p.841D.

9   *Re B (Care: expert witnesses)* [1996] 1FLR 667, Court of Appeal, p.670D.

Building a case

Together with your legal adviser, when you approach a case you should consider step by step how to construct your application and evidence. The following questions need to be considered.

Who has the burden of proof?

If these are care proceedings, the burden rests squarely on the local authority.

What is the standard of proof?

In care proceedings, this is the balance of probabilities, but what does that mean? Is this a case where you have to be especially conscious of *Re H and R* ?

What statutory grounds do you have to prove for the application you are making?

The key Children Act 1989 sections to remember for care proceedings are s38 (interim orders); s31 (threshold criteria for final orders); s1 (welfare principle, welfare checklist, no delay principle and the so-called 'no order principle'); not forgetting all relevant Articles under the Human Rights Act 1998, as well as relevant provisions for any applications you are making under the Adoption and Children Act 2002 (such as a placement order application). Reminding yourself of the statutory grounds helps to focus your mind on what evidence you need to make out your case.

Exactly what is your case to the court in respect of each child individually?

For example, in care proceedings be clear whether you are alleging actual or likely harm, and whether you say this is attributable to inadequate care or lack of control. Precisely what type of harm do you allege? Remember that the grounds must be proven separately in respect of each child – children do not come as a 'job lot'.

What evidence do you have to establish your case?

This is the point at which you need to go from generalised allegations to very specific information illustrating each point. It can help to create a chart or list setting out the allegation, information to support it and where the evidence comes from. For example, one entry for a chart in a general neglect case might be:

Allegation	Supporting information	Source
Inadequate clothing	Child only in T-shirt and nappy on snowy day	Key worker

Who do you have to ask to give evidence, and what kind of evidence can they give?

Who do you need to provide pieces of the jigsaw? Consider everyone involved with the child and family. Agencies might include health (midwives, health visitors, GPs, hospital doctors), education (school teachers, school nurses, teaching assistants, playgroup or nursery staff), police, probation, YOT, adult services (drug or alcohol services, mental health professionals). What factual and opinion evidence can they give?

Do you need to gather any more evidence before the final hearing?

What else do you need to do? Are further assessments or other input needed? Remember to gather updated evidence demonstrating developments as the case progresses, and include evidence from people involved since the case started such as foster carers and contact supervisors.

Is there a need for an expert to carry out a specific assessment for court?

Consider whether you need to instruct someone yourself, or how you would respond to another party seeking an expert opinion.

Conclusion

If you understand the essential rules of evidence and approach the case preparation in an organised, analytical way this can only assist in effective presentation to the court.

Chapter 5

Written Evidence

The importance of written work

When we think about going to court, it is easy to focus on the drama of the day itself, but in fact court work starts long before anyone steps into the witness box. The application and evidence are submitted in writing in advance and are read by the court before anyone gives oral evidence. Presenting your written material well gives you the best chance of persuading the court of the merits of your case, so you owe this to your authority, to the child and to yourself. Of course, even immaculate presentation of a poor case cannot disguise its weakness – but bad presentation can undermine even a good case.

Cases which are soundly based and well presented often settle, saving everyone the stress, time and expense of a court contest. Even if the whole case is not resolved, some witnesses may be excused attendance because their evidence is sufficiently clear from their statements and cross-examination is not required, so by presenting your written work well you may even spare yourself the need to go into the witness box.

If you do have to be called, you give yourself the best start as a witness if you have produced a professional statement. Imagine for a moment a magistrate receiving lever arch files full of documents shortly before a fully contested hearing. It is a daunting task to absorb the information and, being human, he probably has other things he would rather be doing. He comes to the social worker's statement and finds a rambling, disorganised mess which is repetitious, badly presented, difficult to read, full of spelling mistakes and grammatical errors. He is quite likely to abandon it and turn straight to the Guardian's report. When he does plough his way through it, imagine what impression he forms of the social worker and how he feels towards her when she steps into the witness box! In contrast, a statement which is clear, concise, well thought out, logically organised and immaculately presented not only helps the magistrate understand the case but also means that he is well disposed towards the social worker before she even comes to court. This can even go towards building a reputation from one case to another – just as you remember the magistrates, they may remember you.

What considerations do you have to bear in mind?

Deadlines

Any document you produce for court must be on time. As soon as proceedings are underway, a timetable is fixed and deadlines are set for evidence to be filed (delivered to the court) and served (copied to the other parties). This timetable forms part of a court order and must be complied with. If you really cannot keep to a deadline, tell your lawyer in advance so that he can seek an extension of time from the court. Too often, local authority evidence is filed late, and this has a knock-on effect as responses to your evidence are then delayed, and things end up being filed in a rush before the final hearing. Some people (including experts) have such a reputation for being late with their reports that solicitors have been known to give them the wrong date 'accidentally', bringing the deadline forward by a couple of weeks in the hope of getting the report in on time. Avoid gaining such a reputation yourself.

Being late with evidence makes you and your authority look unprofessional and disorganised. Remember that other parties need as much time as possible to absorb your evidence – think, for example, of the illiterate parent for whom everything has to be read out, or a parent with mental health or emotional difficulties, who needs time to take in the information. If professionals cannot stick to a timetable, what chance do they have?

Remember too that other people, including your lawyer, need to check over your evidence before it can be filed and served, so aim to have your work finished at least a few days before it is due in. As soon as directions are given, diarise not just the date your work is due at court, but the date by which it needs to be finished. Put a note in your diary a week, a fortnight and a month before to remind you that the deadline is approaching.

QUESTION FOR REFLECTION

- What habits can you adopt to ensure your work is always on time?

Accuracy

This may seem too obvious to mention, but it is too crucial to omit. Nothing should go into your statement unless you know it to be accurate and truthful. You have to swear to its truth in the witness box and anything untrue could lead to injustice and even to perjury proceedings (just ask Lord Archer) and any number of disciplinary consequences. Don't guess; don't write what you think to be the case without bothering to check. Get it right. If your statement contains errors and inaccuracies, however minor, your credibility and reputation fly swiftly out of the window.

Audience

Consider who will read your work. Whether you are conscious of it or not, you already adjust your writing to its intended audience and purpose – a letter to your Mum is very different from a letter to your bank manager. The people who will read your evidence include:

- your own lawyer, who checks it and refines it to ensure that the case is made out and pitfalls avoided

- the other parties' lawyers, who go through it with a fine-tooth comb looking for gaps, weaknesses, inconsistencies, errors and anything which assists their case

- the other parties themselves, including the parents, who read in detail about their own family and failings, and the Guardian, who analyses your work from a professional standpoint

- the child himself, immediately if he is old enough to take part in the proceedings, or perhaps later when he tries to understand his history

- the court – judge or magistrates – who look for clear evidence and cogent reasoning on which to base the decision.

Think about each of these people when you write and review your statements and reports. How will each of them read it? What will they see in it? Is that what you want them to see?

Types of document

Before you draft any document for court, having a clear idea of its function helps you to produce an effective document. As key worker in care proceedings, you are likely to produce the following documents.

APPLICATION FORMS

These are standard prescribed forms. For care proceedings, complete forms C1 (the general application form) and C13 (the supplement for care proceedings). Follow the instructions on the form and write legibly, in capitals and black ink, remembering that it will be copied umpteen times in the course of the proceedings. The C1 gives necessary basic information including the child's identity, parents' details and local authority details, while the C13 is specific to care proceedings and includes the reasons for the proposed actions. The basis of the case must be clear from these forms, which are the first documents received by the parents and Guardian and their respective solicitors.

SOCIAL WORK CHRONOLOGY

This is filed early in the proceedings, and is updated as the case goes along. It is a skeleton diary of events and should be succinct, identifying key facts on which everyone can agree. It should not contain opinion or judgement; interpretation or analysis should be in a statement, not the chronology. It is effectively a schedule listing dates and events, and if possible should cross-reference to other statements or documents filed.

STATEMENTS OF EVIDENCE

Parties and witnesses file statements of evidence, whereas experts and the Guardian file reports. You are likely to file at least two statements during the case. The initial social work statement has to be produced at the very outset of proceedings, and there may be further interim statements before the final statement. These contain the detailed evidence and analysis in support of your application and explain your recommendation to the court.

INTERIM AND CORE ASSESSMENTS

These are documents which you produce anyway, independent of court proceedings, following a child protection referral and investigation. There is a danger of the same information being repeated ad nauseam between the various documents put before the court. Try to avoid this – repetition bores the reader and tempts him to skim read, bringing the danger that he will skip over something original and important. Instead, cross-reference from one document to another; for example, if the core assessment contains a detailed family history, there is no need to repeat the whole thing in your statement. You could instead summarise the essentials and refer the reader to the relevant section of the assessment for fuller information.

CARE PLANS

Use the format prescribed by the Circular LAC 99(29)[1] for your care plan, which is a crucial document in persuading the court to entrust your authority with a child's future. Each child must have his own individual care plan. It must be countersigned by a senior manager to demonstrate the authority's commitment to see the plan into practice. It is not the place for evidence, which belongs in statements. The self-explanatory main headings are as follows:

---

[1]   Local Authority Circular LAC 99(29) *Care Plans and Care Proceedings under the Children Act 1989.* London: Department of Health.

1. Overall aim.

2. Child's needs including contact.

3. Views of others.

4. Placement details and timetable.

5. Management and support by the local authority (including a contingency plan).

The Circular gives further details of the information expected under each heading. In practice some care plans seem too formulaic with identical plans for different children apparently cut and pasted from one to the other with little thought for the individual child. Each plan should be individual and specific, setting out your authority's realistic intentions for the particular child.

Statement content

Obviously the precise content depends on the detail of your particular case and you need to work closely with your lawyer to get this right. You also need to be clear about your role in the case – are you a witness of fact or are you also qualified to give opinions? Are you giving evidence about a discrete piece of work, such as contact observation, or are you the key worker putting forward the case as a whole? If your evidence just relates to one piece of work, stick to that and do not stray beyond your boundaries. The rest of this section applies primarily to the key worker.

Initial statement

An initial statement is, by necessity, different in content from a final one. By definition it comes at the very outset of proceedings when the court and the other parties know nothing of your case. You therefore need to set the scene clearly. What has prompted the proceedings? What is the essential background to the case and the key information about the child and family? What have Social Services done so far? What do you propose to do from here?

Sometimes, proceedings follow a long stretch of work with a child and family. You might have been working for months to avoid the need for proceedings and already have completed a full core assessment – if so, file it with the court straight away. You can give the court full information from the start, and there may not be much further assessment work to be done in the course of proceedings.

However, the situation is quite different in a case which starts as an emergency (such as a serious physical injury), where you have no previous knowledge of the family. Then your initial statement is necessarily sparse and can only give the information available to date, including as much detail as possible on the incident which propelled you to court, any emergency action taken, other known court cases or orders relating to the child, and such background as you have on the family, including your initial assessment.

The court clearly needs to know essential details about the child – age, sex, significant cultural factors, disabilities or special vulnerability. Much assessment work remains to be done during the proceedings, so the court needs to know your plans, who is to do what and when. At this early stage, you have to use your crystal ball and anticipate foreseeable contingencies.

If your plan involves removing the child from home, an initial care plan is also needed, with as much detail as possible as to placement and contact.

This initial statement differs considerably from a final statement written after months of proceedings, hours of assessments and volumes of evidence. Generally speaking, the initial statement focuses more on facts, while the final statement has greater emphasis on the analysis of the whole case, leading to a final proposal to the court.

What does the court need?

Whenever you write a statement, think about what the judge or magistrate needs, remembering that what you do not tell him he will not know. If you were the judge, what information would you want from the key worker? You might ask the following questions:

WHO ARE YOU? WHAT IS YOUR ROLE AND WHY SHOULD I LISTEN TO YOU?

Start your first statement with your full name and professional address (never reveal your personal contact details), and job title (including a very brief explanation if necessary). Give your qualifications and experience to establish your entitlement to give opinion evidence. Some pre-qualification experience and other activities can be relevant and should be included. Some witnesses overdo it, including membership of organisations for which only a subscription is required – no one is fooled by this and it tends to undermine the value of the other entries in the list. A long list of letters after your name does not assist the court either – be prepared to explain those which are not obvious.

Do not trawl through your full details in every statement you write for the same case – this wastes time and energy and no one will read it a second time. After the first statement just give your name and address and refer to the details of your qualifications and experience in your first statement, giving its date. Do, however, add details if you have subsequently been promoted or obtained a further qualification.

State your role with the family and consider including a brief explanation of what this actually entails, how often you visit and how you work. Social workers sometimes complain that they are given less credence than the Guardian even though they know the child and family better. This may be because they are not giving the court enough information. In their reports, Guardians detail every interview undertaken and are precise about who they have seen and when, but social workers are not always so exact if asked for the same details. Can you say how often you have visited a family you are working with or how long you have spent with the child? If not, why not? Support your claim to know the family well by including details in your statement. This was important in one interim hearing where the Guardian disagreed with the local authority's application. The social worker believed that the Guardian did not have a true picture of the family, who had put on a show for her, and that the child had not told her his real feelings. The social worker was able to tell the court that she had worked with the family over three months, clocking up 24 hours with the parents and a further 18 hours with the child individually. In contrast, the Guardian had spent a total of 1½ hours with the family and had seen the child once. The court preferred the social worker's evidence.

WHAT ARE YOU ASKING ME TO DO?

This is not a thriller where you build up the suspense to the end before revealing your application. Be clear at the outset what your application is and what order(s) (interim or final) you seek. Your reasoning and analysis come later, but stating early on exactly what you seek allows the court and other parties to read your statement in context.

WHO IS THIS CASE ABOUT?

The child's basic details (name, sex, date of birth) should appear early on in your first statement, and you should make sure that you include all relevant details about the child's background and characteristics. Once, a judge who had read all of the papers before a first hearing was surprised to see a black mother and white father in court – the child's mixed racial heritage appeared nowhere in the papers. When you work closely on a case, it is sometimes easy to overlook what seems obvious to you – don't forget the court does not know unless you tell it.

Try to convey a picture of the child as a person. It is too easy for paper-based professionals (such as lawyers and judges) to regard the child as simply the subject of the proceedings, an object of concern, not an individual. We focus on what has happened to the child and his problems, and rarely get a glimpse of personality, let alone talents or interests.

Remember also always to bring the evidence back to the child – too often cases focus on adults, the local authority concentrating on the parents' inadequacies and the parents complaining about Social Services. The only reason why any of the information about the parents' background, lifestyle or behaviour is relevant is because of its impact on the child, whose welfare is paramount. Sometimes it is useful to remind yourself why you are putting information in. The mother's heroin addiction is there not because you disapprove of drug use, nor even because it is harming her health – the only reason it matters to you or the court is because it harms her child.

WHO ARE THE CHILD'S PARENTS, AND WHAT IS THE FAMILY STRUCTURE?

Identify at an early stage who is who in the child's life. Make it clear who the parents are and who has parental responsibility. Never overlook the child's father even if he does not live with the family. If he has parental responsibility, he is automatically a party to the proceedings and must be served with all the papers. Even if he does not have parental responsibility, he cannot be ignored – some cases have gone right through to adoption proceedings before the putative father has been contacted, only to find he or his family want to care for the child, causing delay and trauma to all concerned. Tell the court what you know about the child's paternity and what efforts you have made or will make to track the father down. If there is any doubt, DNA testing is now cheap, simple and effective.

Siblings and half-siblings must not be overlooked. Care planning can become complex particularly where large age gaps, different parentage or other considerations lead to different plans for siblings, and these issues should be identified early on.

Some families are very complicated – we have all encountered the family of six children with three different fathers, one of whom also has children with the mother's sister. In such cases a diagram such as a family tree or genogram can help to explain the family structure.

WHAT HARM DO YOU SAY THIS CHILD IS SUFFERING OR IS AT RISK OF SUFFERING?

You should be able to give a clear, concise summary of why the case is in court. Do you allege actual or likely harm, is it physical, sexual or emotional harm and is it through abuse or neglect?

WHAT IS YOUR EVIDENCE FOR YOUR ALLEGATIONS?

This is obviously the meat of the statement and is the longest element. You need to substantiate, illustrate and justify your case with relevant information put into context.

Concentrate on your own direct evidence, using hearsay only where necessary. As key worker, you can refer to statements from others (without repeating the detail) to show how the case fits together as a whole.

Make sure you convey your key points clearly and that the balance is right. Important issues must be given appropriate detail and emphasis; trivial points might be left out altogether. Sometimes the balance is wrong – one statement mentioned a child's worryingly sexualised behaviour in one sentence, but spent a page and a half on the dangers of passive smoking! In another case of gross neglect the social worker complained in her statement that the mother had not washed her curtains. Several professionals in the case were left guiltily wondering when they had last washed their own curtains! It does not help to throw in every single criticism of the parent or family – in fact it gives the impression either of muddled thinking ('this worker doesn't know what's important') or judgemental hyper-criticism ('this poor mother can't do anything right'). Does it really matter? Can the child stay at home if her parents continue to smoke, or if the curtains are chronically unclean? Focus on what really needs to change.

Give specific examples and illustrations, avoiding generalised comments and subjective judgments (words like 'unacceptable' or 'inappropriate'). Once a social worker discussing potential proceedings explained to her lawyer that the home conditions were unsuitable. The lawyer asked for clarification. The worker explained that the hygiene standards were unacceptably poor. The lawyer asked for facts not an opinion. The discussion continued in the same vein until the worker, exasperated, said 'look, the other day I went in and the sink was full of washing up with a dishcloth on top. Mother took the dishcloth, wiped the baby's bottom then put the cloth back in the sink.' At last the lawyer was happy – with factual evidence like that, the magistrates could work out for themselves that this was poor hygienic practice. Paint the picture for the court – don't forget the magistrates will never visit the home, meet the child or see the family in action.

Give detailed observations of family interactions, rather than simply expressing a view of the strength of attachments – show the court where you get your opinions from.

Consider whether to attach anything to your statement; this is known as an 'exhibit'. If you have referred to a written agreement, attach a copy. If you have gone through a workbook or have produced charts, daily programmes, lists of targets or any other tool in your work with the family, consider whether a copy would help the court. Don't forget photographs or evidence other than the written word.

WHAT ARE THE FAMILY'S STRENGTHS?

You swear to tell the court the whole truth – not just the bits of the truth which suit your case. The local authority must give the court the full picture, and not drive forward towards its desired conclusion, presenting information selectively. Judges have often stressed the importance of balance. For example Wall J (now LJ) said in *Re JC*[2]:

> All parties have a duty in family proceedings not to be tendentious in the presentation of their evidence. That duty is, however, particularly acute in relation to local authority evidence, and never more so than when the local authority is advising the court of its view of the outcome of an assessment of parental capacity or otherwise setting out its recommendations and plans. The duty of local authorities to be objective, fair and balanced cannot be overemphasised.

If you fail to heed this advice, the parents' advocates will inevitably cross-examine you to elicit all of their clients' positive qualities. The next question is why none of these were in your statement. If you have left out these important matters, what else have you also conveniently omitted to mention? You are made to look biased, judgemental and selective – not a witness the court would choose to trust. Far better, therefore, to be fair and balanced throughout. Although we can all think of a few clients about whom it is a struggle to find positive comments, most families have strengths as well as weaknesses and although the negatives may outweigh the positives, both need to be stated.

WHAT HAVE SOCIAL SERVICES DONE?

The court needs to know what your department and other agencies have done to try to improve things. This goes towards explaining why an order is necessary.

Just as the parents are not without redeeming features, it is unlikely that Social Services are beyond reproach. Imagine a hypothetical case where timely action has not been taken, the case has languished unallocated, a service was unavailable due to lack of resources or in some other way your department has failed to cover itself with glory. How do you handle it? Essentially you have two options: say nothing and hope that no one notices, or tackle it head on.

If you say nothing, how likely is it that the lawyers and the court will all miss the point? If one of them does take the matter up, you will immediately be on the defensive, as if you had tried to hide something, and again the implication arises that there might be other things you have conveniently omitted. It looks as though the barrister has winkled information out of you, and has scored a point. He will make a meal of it. Your confidence will be undermined and your department's credibility damaged.

2   Re JC *(Care proceedings)* [1995] 2 FLR 77, High Court Family Division, p.80D.

In contrast, if you tackle the issue yourself, acknowledging the failings in your statement (without blowing them out of proportion), apologising if necessary, then moving on, you are demonstrably being frank with the court and fair to all parties.

There is nothing wrong with acknowledging, for example, that, with hindsight, there might have been grounds for proceedings long ago but they were not taken through a desire, perhaps misplaced, to keep the child at home if at all possible. The fact that it could be argued that action should have been taken earlier is not a reason to compound the error by continuing to fail to act.

What can the other parties do with their criticism now? They can still make the same points, but much of the sting has been drawn. Their criticisms are not original, and the social worker can refer to the acknowledgment already in her statement. By so doing, she clearly shows her honesty and fairness, and is likely to win the court's respect.

WHAT IS YOUR PROFESSIONAL OPINION?

As you go through the facts of the case, if necessary and where appropriate, apply your professional expertise to explain the significance of the factual evidence or help the court interpret the information.

WHAT STATUTORY CRITERIA DO YOU WANT ME TO APPLY?

This obviously depends on what order you seek, so you need to work with your lawyer on this section. At the interim stage, you need to refer to s38 Children Act 1989, but in your final statement this section will be much fuller. You need to consider the full threshold criteria set out in s31 Children Act 1989 and to analyse the welfare principle (s1(1)) and 'welfare checklist' (s1(3)), as well as considering the so-called 'no order principle' (s1(5)). If you are also applying for an order (such as a placement order) under the Adoption and Children Act 2002 you should address those criteria too. Never forget the Human Rights Act 1998, which should be at the forefront of your professional consciousness throughout your practice in any event. Explaining in your statement how you have taken it into account pre-empts any possibility of a smart barrister implying that you have failed to consider the issue of respect for family life.

WHAT IS YOUR CONCLUSION AND RECOMMENDATION?

This is your opportunity to sum up your evidence and recommendations, clearly showing the link between the factual information and the conclusion you ask the court to reach.

When you first receive a report, do you start at the beginning and read to the end, or do you, like many of us, turn straight to the last paragraph and read the conclusion first, only then going back to read the rest? Bear in mind that at least some of your readers, possibly the judge himself, will read your conclusion first. Make sure it stands alone and is clear, concise and well reasoned.

Research

Social workers often ask whether they should refer in evidence to research or the theoretical basis for their opinions. Practice is increasingly research and evidence based, and the drive to increase the professionalism of social work includes the Change Project 'Research Evidence in the Family Court' established by Research in Practice.[3]

Nonetheless, take care before you cite research or theory. Ask yourself whether it is necessary at all – most care cases proceed without it. Is the point so unusual and technical that it needs to be justified? Have you actually used the research or theory in your work with the child? If not, it is no good producing it just for court to look more professional – you will regret it when it comes to cross-examination. Always consider how the research or theory relates to this child and this family; generalisations do not assist the court.

If you do consider it essential, be very careful. One problem is that whatever research you cite, someone else will find a study supporting the opposite proposition, and that 'someone else' is quite likely to be the parents' barrister! You therefore need to know if there are any contradictory opinions and to be able to explain why you discount them.

Make sure any theoretical work you rely on is sound and respectable – just as with any other expert, if you take a view which is not generally accepted within your profession, you must acknowledge that upfront; court is not a place to crusade for unorthodox or innovative beliefs. Work funded or published by government departments or well known institutions is likely to be safe – your friend's doctoral thesis is not.

Beware of the internet. In one case, a research paper was produced, obtained from the internet, propounding an original theory that would explain a child's medical symptoms. When the source was investigated, it transpired that the writer was a doctor – but in geography – and other papers on the same site included accounts of alien abductions. If you do find information to support your case, follow it up, authenticate it and analyse it – imagine the questions a sharp, well-informed lawyer will ask and make sure you have the answers. It is perfectly legitimate for the other parties to ask for a copy of anything you rely on, so make sure you can provide it at short notice or, better still, supply it in advance.

---

3   Research in Practice is a Department of the Dartington Hall Trust. Accessed on 1/5/07 at http://www.rip.org.uk/changeprojects/evidencecourt.asp.

If (and only if) research really is necessary, and you present it properly, it could add to your credibility as a witness – but do it carelessly and you will undermine your own professionalism. Avoid at all costs generalised statements such as 'we know from research…' – that is simply asking for trouble.

QUESTION FOR REFLECTION

- How can your department build up a database of reliable research information including information about possible counter-arguments?

Chapter 6

Statement Presentation

Presentation matters

Deciding on the content of your statement is half the battle; you then need to get the information across effectively. This includes using the right format, organising the material and expressing yourself clearly and appropriately.

Format

There are formal requirements for court documents and complying with these is essential for professional presentation. In the case of statements, these are set out in the court rules (Family Proceedings Rules 1991 in the County and High Court, Family Proceedings Courts Rules 1991 for the FPC).

Box 6.1: Family Proceedings Rules 1991 r 4.17

(1) ... a party shall file and serve on the parties, any welfare officer and any guardian ad litem...

(a) written statements of the substance of the oral evidence which the party intends to adduce at a hearing of, or a directions appointment in, whose proceedings, which shall –

  (i) be dated,

  (ii) be signed by the person making the statement,

  (iii) contain a declaration that the maker of the statement believes it to be true and understands that it may be placed before the court; and

  (iv) show in the top right hand corner of the first page –

    (a) the initials and surname of the person making the statement,

---

> (b) the number of the statement in relation to the maker,
>
> (c) the date on which the statement was made, and
>
> (d) the party on whose behalf it is filed; and
>
> (b) copies of any documents, including experts' reports, upon which the party intends to rely at a hearing of, or a directions appointment in, those proceedings, at or by, such time as the court directs or, in the absence of a direction, before the hearing or appointment...
>
> (3) At a hearing or a directions appointment a party may not, without the leave of the court –
>
> (a) adduce evidence, or
>
> (b) seek to rely on a document,
>
> in respect of which he has failed to comply with the requirements of paragraph (1).[1]

Never forget the case number. Children's cases are always classified by their numbers and names are not read out in order to preserve confidentiality. Get the number wrong and the document may never reach the correct file.

Use A4 paper and type on one side only. Allow sufficient margins so that the statement can be photocopied and hole-punched without chopping off part of the text. Use at least 1 and a half line spacing. Number all paragraphs – you will be grateful for this when you are referred to the text in the witness box – it is much easier to find 'paragraph 5' than 'the 23rd line, about three-quarters of the way down the page', especially when you are nervous! Keep the numbering style consistent throughout. If you start with 1 (a) and (b), don't suddenly change to 2.1 part way through.

Organisation

You have a lot of important information to convey in a limited space. It can only be accessible if it is well organised.

Consider the judge and the other parties. They need to be able to read the statement through from beginning to end and make sense of it, but also to find their way to relevant information when they need it. Imagine that, in the heat of the hearing, a witness says something untrue (e.g. the mother says she attended

3   Office of Public Sector Information (1991) *Family Proceedings Rules.* London: OPSI. Accessed on 1/5/07 at http://www.opsi.gov.uk/SI/si199112.htm

a particular meeting whereas your statement says she did not). It is no good having your advocate fumbling around thinking 'I know I read that somewhere'; he needs to be able to turn straight to the details in your statement to challenge her evidence, so a clear structure is crucial.

Box 6.2: Making information accessible

Give yourself 15 seconds each to read A and B

A. It might be possible to argue that the layout and appearance of a statement should not be considered as particularly important; rather that the content of the statement is the only significant matter. Arguably, however, the problem is that the content of the statement can only be appreciated if the reader can actually read and absorb it. If the page is too tightly packed with small, closely spaced verbiage lacking any divisions which might assist the reader by separating the text into manageable sections and failing to provide headings which might help in anticipating and understanding the main topics and structure of the statement, and if the text consists of very long sentences, repetitions and unnecessary verbiage, as well as multiple sub-clauses which are simply too complex and serve only to obscure the content of the sentence, set within extremely long paragraphs, then ultimately the sense of the text becomes lost and the effort put into writing the statement becomes wasted as the meaning is obscured. It can actually be physically difficult and tiring to read if the writing is too small and too closely packed together, especially when this continues for page after page. It can even be difficult to follow the sense of the writing, and sometimes one can get the feeling that the writer him or herself has actually got lost, followed inevitably by the reader! If the reader has to read a sentence or a paragraph more than once to try to find the sense of it, then the writer has wasted his or her time. The chances are that the reader will not make the effort to keep on trying and will move on. If the sentence or paragraph had obscured within it important information, then that information itself is passed over. Further, it is simply unappealing and does not entice the reader, who may already be reluctant, tired or bored, to want to read the text and he or she will be encouraged to skim over all or part of the text or alternatively to find another statement (or perhaps the Guardian's report) to read instead. Surprising as it may seem to many, judges and magistrates are in fact human, and do not differ greatly from other readers. It is difficult to justify writing a statement in a way which makes life more difficult for the reader or in a way which the writer him or herself would in fact be reluctant to read were the positions reversed.

B. The layout of a statement is important because its content will only be noticed if it is accessible.

Possible problems with statements include:

- font too small
- line spacing too close
- lack of sub-divisions and headings
- unnecessarily complex sentences
- excessively long paragraphs.

Small writing is difficult and tiring to read. Complex sentences can obscure the meaning and bore the reader. Large blocks of dense text are unattractive and discourage the reader.

Why write a statement you would not want to read yourself?

Social work statements can sometimes read like amplified chronologies and simply trawl through every single contact with the family and every step taken, in great detail. This makes turgid reading and leaves the reader to do the work in figuring out the significance of each event. It can be better to organise the information by topics rather than dates, bearing in mind that the court already has your social work chronology. Sometimes lists or bullet points can make points more clearly than long screeds of text.

Headings and sub-headings give structure to your statement, breaking up the text into manageable chunks and providing helpful signposting for the reader. Put all your points about the same topic in the same section. Use different typefaces for clarification, such as bold for headings or italics for quotations.

Sentences should be of a manageable length, without too many sub-clauses. This is in your own interests, as well as those of your readers, as if you are referred to your statement in the witness box, you will live to regret long and complex sentences. Experts in plain English recommend that sentences should generally contain one main point and should not be too long – aim for 40 words as a maximum and 15–20 words as an average. This makes the content more easily accessible. However, you do need to vary sentence length a little, or the statement will seem too staccato and will not flow. Collect sentences on the same topic into paragraphs, which also need to be of a sensible length.

Length

Social workers sometimes ask how long a statement should be. There is no easy answer; much, of course, depends on the characteristics of the particular case. There is also a question of personal style – some people are more concise than others and, even given the same facts and the same conclusion, no two people would write the same statement. You know whether you naturally are verbose or concise. If you tend to write too much, write a first draft then edit it. Always ask yourself why each piece of information you are giving is relevant – what does it add? Remove sentences which add nothing or if what they do add does not need saying.

Imagine you are packing for a plane journey with a strict baggage weight allowance: you probably over-pack to start with, then you prune, leaving behind the unnecessary items, reducing the number of similar things, or replacing several items altogether with a single more useful one. You can apply the same ideas to your writing.

If you need to become more concise, try practising a précis exercise. Take a passage of, say, 150 words from a book or journal and try to rewrite it in 100 words, or 50 words (the word count facility in word processing packages is a godsend). This sharpens the discipline of analysing the key points in the text, then expressing those ideas more economically, discarding the excess baggage along the way. You can then use these skills in your statement writing.

It is equally possible to be too brief and too sparse. Too little information can even be worse than being too long-winded. The waffler risks boring the reader and losing important points in a welter of unnecessary detail, but the taciturn writer could fail even to make the case or, if she adds further information in the witness box which was not in the statement, could be criticised for apparently trying to surprise the opposition with new information. Sometimes a case which is long and complex requires a long and complex statement – as Einstein put it: 'make it as simple as possible, but no simpler'.

Language

Language should be formal but plain and clear – use ordinary English words without patronising your audience. Avoid jargon and be prepared to explain any specialist terms you do use. However, don't lose sight of common sense – the health visitor service which appended a 'glossary of specialist terms' to statements really did not need to explain that 'pregnancy' was a term meaning 'the period of gestation of the foetus prior to birth'!

Use language which is natural to you, albeit the formal version of you – do not try to impress with your learning, and never use a word unless you are completely sure of its meaning. You could end up being cross- examined about why you have chosen a particular word or expressed yourself in a particular way and it is difficult to answer if you have written in a way which is unnatural to you. In the old days of wardship, social workers' affidavits were often drafted by lawyers, not by the workers themselves. One worker found herself in the witness box asked repeatedly about why she had used a particular term in her affidavit. She struggled gamely to answer the question several times but when it was posed yet again she gave up in exasperation, saying, 'I don't know, I didn't write it – she did!' and pointed to the lawyer at the back of the court.

Parents' solicitors have a difficult task preparing their clients' evidence. Most parents are not equipped to draft their own statements, so solicitors have do it for them, trying to get the parents' point across in language they might use, although sometimes with necessary editing! Occasionally parents' statements contain patent lawyer-speak, such as 'I have been informed and verily believe' or 'I deny each and every allegation made by the local authority and I put them to strict proof thereof'. Most advocates resist the temptation to cross-examine the parents on what they meant by those words. Although your lawyer is unlikely to make such clumsy changes to your statement, words or sentences inserted by someone else might stand out because of a difference in style. It is better for them to suggest the sense of the alteration and let you write it in your own words.

Guides to plain English generally advise writers to use the active ('the fostering officer will support the placement') rather than the passive voice ('the placement will be supported by the fostering officer').

Sometimes social workers write in the third person, referring to themselves as 'the social worker' rather in the style of a doctoral thesis ('the writer will demonstrate'). However, a social work statement which says, for example, 'the social worker went to the house' is unclear – it raises the question of 'which social worker?' It can sound pretentious or give the impression that the writer is trying to disown the action. One of the give-away signs that a worker does not agree with actions taken is when she writes, for example, 'the Department decided', thereby distancing herself from the decision. It is far better and clearer to write about your own actions in the first person ('I went to the house').

Grammar and spelling

Our education system has not always laid great store on grammar or spelling, on occasions preferring to encourage self-expression. As a result, even some highly educated people make basic errors. Court proceedings are not English language exams but spelling and grammar still matter. Mistakes can change the sense of a sentence. Look at the following two sentences – only the punctuation changes, but the sense is completely different: The client said the social worker was a bitch; or 'The client,' said the social worker, 'was a bitch.'

A statement which contains errors of whatever nature looks unprofessional. Remember your audience and bear in mind that judges in particular tend to come from a narrow social group often educated in a traditional manner, and, being lawyers, also tend to be pedantic.

Some people are driven to distraction by common grammatical errors such as the split infinitive ('to boldly go') or the greengrocers' (or is it greengrocer's?) apostrophe (pear's 30p). However irrational it may seem to those more relaxed about such things, some people presented with a statement full of such errors can barely see past them to the content. If you are not confident about the difference between *it's* and *its*, *parents*, *parent's* and *parents'* or *there*, *their* and *they're*, the office assistant on your computer may help, but remember that the computer is no substitute for a thinking human being – ask a colleague well-versed in grammar to check your work for you, and consider brushing up your skills.

Names

When you write about adults, as a general rule you should use their title and surname, at least on the first occasion. This shows an appropriate level of formality and respect for the individual concerned. If you find this artificial, you could, for example, write 'the child's mother is Mrs Jane Smith, who I will refer to in this statement as "Jane" as we work together on first name terms'. This explains to the court that you are not using her first name because you regard yourself as superior to her, and that she uses your first name as well – you don't expect her to call you 'Madam'!

Be aware that different cultures have different naming systems and do not always have a first name followed by a surname. Be particularly careful to get it right, and if in doubt, ask the people themselves for the correct form of address.

Be careful to differentiate if there is more than one family member with the same name.

Always take care to spell names correctly, particularly if the spellings are idiosyncratic. Many people are justifiably highly offended by mistakes in their name, and it does imply a lack of care and respect. Surnames can be a major bone of contention – many private law disputes centre on a child's surname, and courts take the issue of children's names very seriously – so make sure you get it right. Dates of birth also matter. Parents can become very upset about mistakes of this kind, even when they accept damning criticism of their behaviour without apparent demur. It can also put you on the back foot in the witness box, apologising for an error before you have even started, and what may seem a relatively minor matter can be blown out of all proportion, denting your confidence.

Avoid referring to parties as 'the mother / father' (unless you genuinely do not know their names). It comes across as dismissive, not to say plain rude.

Sensitivity

Remember that the people you are writing about (parents and children) are likely to read your work and, unlike others in the case, you will carry on working with them after the court proceedings are over. It is essential to be frank about events in the family and this necessarily involves raising sensitive issues, detailing very personal matters and analysing people's failings. These matters must be tackled head-on without pussy-footing around or you will not convey your concerns to the court. However, there is no need to be gratuitous or insensitive. For example, one report included the fact that the mother's false teeth fell out during an interview. Another report described a father as a 'psychosexual deviant' because he was gay. Expressing things in this way hardly assisted the court in its task and was unnecessarily hurtful to the individuals involved. Imagine also the impression of the writer this conveys to the court – is someone who writes like this a fair-minded, sensitive professional? How, then, has he worked with this family and what attitude has he taken towards them? How reliable are his recommendations to the court?

There is nothing wrong with expressing regret, sympathy or sadness in a statement, where appropriate. A case where the parents' inadequate care for the child is due to their learning disabilities is very different from a case of sadistic cruelty and it is perfectly proper for the statements to reflect this. In the first case, it is quite appropriate to comment, for example, that despite the parents' evident love for the child and the authority's efforts to support them, sadly they have proved unable to provide good enough care. The parents' pain and sadness at being separated from their child should be acknowledged. A statement does not have to be cold and impersonal to be professional.

Emotive language

A judge hearing a Guardian describe a case as the worst she had ever seen commented, 'Yes, it always is, isn't it?' The Guardian had said the same thing so many times that it was simply devalued, like the boy who cried 'wolf'. When the day came when she was confronted with a truly awful situation, she had no words left to convey it.

Avoid overstatement and absolutes – be careful about 'always', 'never' or any sense of 100 per cent certainty. Words like 'appalling', 'disgusting', 'shocking' are emotional, emotive and subjective. They may tell the court more about the writer than about the situation described. You are not writing a novel; your aim is not to provoke an emotional response from the reader. If such words are to be used at all, they should be saved for truly exceptional situations which really merit them. Even then, sometimes cool understatement is more effective than emotive language. Read the Climbié report[2] and the descriptions of events. You will not find adjectives; they are not necessary. The bare facts say it all.

Tone

The same information can be expressed in countless ways, each with a different nuance; it is not just what you say, but how you say it that matters. The English language is particularly rich, having numerous synonyms and words with only subtly different meaning. A thesaurus can be very useful to help you find just the right word.

Always remember that the way you write not only conveys information about your subject matter, but also about you. Your readers form impressions of you and your practice, which they will take with them into court before you even set foot in the witness box.

Box 6.3: Choosing the right word

The following words could all be used to describe a 13-year-old. What different impressions do they convey? Which might you choose to use and why?

- child
- youth
- juvenile
- young person
- teenager
- adolescent
- schoolboy/girl
- youngster
- kid.

Reactions to the list vary, and it is very much a matter of personal taste, but some comments follow:

---

2   Laming (2003) *The Victoria Climbié Inquiry: Report of an Inquiry by Lord Laming.* London: Stationery Office. Accessed on 19/1/07 at http://www.victoria-climbie-inquiry.org.uk.

Child This is legally correct as childhood lasts until 18. Most people, however, instinctively feel that 'child' refers to someone younger than 13. A worker might choose this word deliberately, for example, for a 13-year-old who appears streetwise and acts like an older teenager to remind everyone he is in fact a child. The same point might be made for a 13-year-old who has an inappropriate level of responsibility, caring for siblings or incapacitated parents.

Youth If used as a noun ('a youth') people generally think male not female, and the tone is critical not positive – it implies trouble, as in 'a group of youths', conjuring up an image of a gang hanging around menacingly on a street corner. As an adjective, it might summon up 'youth court', but can also be positive, as in 'youth orchestra' or 'youth group'.

Juvenile The universal reaction to this word is that it is negative in tone and masculine in gender.

Young person Professionals like this term. It seems respectful of the individual, acknowledging his status as a person, just a youthful one. Some young people themselves, however, find it patronising (or, in the words of one teenage client, 'poncey'). It is an artificial term, not one the average person would use, and borders on jargon. Young woman/man or girl/boy might be more natural.

Teenager Reactions to this are mixed. For a 13-year-old, becoming a teenager is an important milestone. Some, however, think of 'Kevin' (Harry Enfield's teenage comic creation).

Adolescent This often suggests a medical context (particularly child and adolescent mental health services) and does accurately label the phase between childhood and adulthood, but it also raises the spectre of hormones, mood swings and acne. It rarely conjures up a positive image.

Schoolboy/girl Generally this creates an image of a younger child, and a picture of innocence. It is notable that often the media refer to child victims of crime as, for example, 'the murdered schoolgirl' even where there is no connection between the crime and school. It seems that this is precisely to convey the impression of innocence betrayed.

Youngster Often this is thought to give the impression of an older speaker. Some find it patronising, others consider it affectionate.

Kid A word you might use informally but not in a report. For some this raises hackles, but this is how some young clients describe themselves.

This exercise shows that the choice of which noun is used conveys a different picture of the same person.

Box 6.4: Choosing the right tone

Here are three descriptions of the same person. What do they convey to you?

1. John is a young person with a problem of drug use, leading to repeated involvement in criminal activity. He needs help with anger management.

2. John is a repeat offender and drug abuser with low impulse control.

3. John is a drug-addicted thug.

The three descriptions give similar information, but in very different ways. Example 1 takes care first to describe John as a young person before detailing his problems. The other two examples both label him by his behaviour. Example 1 identifies the underlying problem, then the consequence, then suggests assistance. Neither of the others suggests any constructive response to the situation. Then there is the difference in language, example 1 being moderate and mild, example 2 using labels, and straying into jargon (especially 'low impulse control') whereas example 3 is colloquial. It has been suggested that example 1 is what the social worker writes for care proceedings, 2 is for the Youth Court and 3 is what she says in the office.

Perhaps the most notable difference, however, is the difference in tone between the three examples. As well as gaining information about John, you have probably formed an impression of the author of each statement, her attitudes and approach.

Critical reading

Try reviewing statements you have written in the past, and consider statements produced by others. Read them critically and think how they could be improved.

Top ten writing tips

1. Make time to write

It is simply impossible to write a good statement in ten minutes here and there snatched between other appointments. You need to allow a good stretch of uninterrupted time to do justice to the task. Effectively, writing time has to be treated as any other professional commitment such as a meeting or appointment. Strike the time out in your diary and ensure that both you and your colleagues treat this as sacrosanct, not a luxury.

2. Find space to write

You need a quiet space to work where you can concentrate uninterrupted. Some people work well at home, while others suddenly feel an overwhelming need to clean the oven – you know what works for you. Take care also to preserve confidentiality if you work at home, including computer security. If you have to work at the office find a quiet room. Some teams who have no option but to work in an open plan office use a 'traffic light' system, with red, amber and green symbols on their desks, indicating to colleagues what level of emergency justifies an interruption – writing a statement is definitely 'code red' (do not disturb except in case of fire).

3. Re-read your file

Before you start to write, refresh your memory of the file, including related files. This may be a lot of reading, but over time details fade from memory. Sometimes you will see a pattern when you look back over the whole story which was not apparent at the time, or you may gain a new perspective on a case you thought you already knew. Take the opportunity to ensure that your file is in good order and to flag up important pages ready for the court day.

4. Think

It sounds too obvious to mention but you need to be very clear in your own mind exactly what you want to say before you commit it to paper. Often we are so pressed, rushing from one appointment to the next, that we have little time for reflection. You cannot write coherently without first formulating your thoughts. Simple steps like sorting out in your own mind the three most important things that need to change to allow the child to stay at home can help.

5. Plan

Once you know what you want to say, the next stage is to plan how to say it. Time spent planning saves time writing and if you try to write without planning, you are likely to produce an unstructured stream of consciousness. Refine your thinking – plan your structure and be clear of the major points you want to get across. Many people find it useful to write down their headings before they start on the content.

6. Get started

Procrastination is a common problem. Sometimes we say we haven't got time to do one thing yet manage to find time to do something else, so it can be a question of priorities. Everyone appreciates that social workers have heavy workloads, but it is difficult to think of anything more important than proceedings which could determine a child's future. If you genuinely cannot find time for this important task, you have a more profound problem – either your workload is too heavy, or you are not coping effectively with it and need some support or training such as a time management course. Either way, you owe it to yourself and your clients to tackle this with your seniors.

Why do you procrastinate? Is it because you think you work better under pressure, so (consciously or not) effectively ensure that you have no choice but to work up to the last minute? If so, it might help to break down the task into chunks and set deadlines for sections of work, rather than producing the whole thing in a rush, which is likely to lead to poor work.

Often, we put off daunting tasks, perhaps through an unconscious fear of failure, so avoiding the issue altogether seems a better option, at least for a while. Perhaps we simply do not know where to start, so we postpone the task in the hope that inspiration will strike or something will happen to make it easier. The job then becomes increasingly intimidating as it gets more urgent – we get trapped in a vicious circle. When we finally make a start, we usually find it is nothing like as difficult as we had built it up to be. The key is to face the challenge and make a start. If you do so early, you can get help along the way.

If you know you tend to procrastinate, you need to make it harder for yourself to avoid the problem than to tackle it – ask a colleague to nag you, or programme your computer to give you irritating reminders, so you have the extra motivation to get them 'off your back'. Sometimes it helps to have a treat or reward in store for completing the work, or even staged mini-rewards for finishing each section.

7. *Write out of order if necessary*

Word processors mean that we are no longer bound to write documents starting at the beginning and continuing slavishly to the end. If you get stuck on a particular section, move on and come back to it later. Just as some of us read the conclusion of a report first, some people write it first, finding this helps ensure that the statement as a whole works logically towards that reasoned conclusion. Others prefer to start with the easier sections – personal details, family structure; this can be encouraging as the word count rises quickly.

Often it is worth writing something, even if you know it is not perfect. It is better to have something to work on, amend, re-word and get help with than to have everything swimming around in your head.

8. *Don't rely too much on computers*

Marvellous as they are, computers can also be the source of errors.

If you cut and paste, remember to read the paragraphs before and after the moved section to ensure it flows as a whole, and that there is no change of tense, terminology or style from one paragraph to the next. Make sure numbers still follow in the correct order and check that the layout is not disrupted causing, for example, disembodied headings to appear at the foot of the page.

Sometimes it is tempting to borrow a sentence or paragraph from another report you have written, or perhaps a colleague's statement which you find effective. Make sure this fits with the rest of the statement – a sudden change of style or tone can jar. Students are often amazed that their tutors can spot plagiarism, but sometimes a section of published text is inserted word for word into the student's work and the reader immediately and instinctively feels the abrupt change.

If you copy a paragraph relating to one child into a document about another, check very carefully to ensure that the name is changed every single time. In care plans where the plans for siblings are practically identical, it is sometimes apparent that the worker drafted the care plan for the oldest then simply re-hashed it for the younger children. Too often, one child's name slips into a plan supposedly about a different child. This smacks of a lack of care, even a lack of importance accorded to the second child, implying that the children are treated as a 'job lot'. Tempting as it is to save time, consider very carefully whether the words you have used are just as appropriate for one child as for the other.

Spell checks can be helpful, but remember that they sometimes offer American spellings and they cannot spot mistakes which still result in real words, which can entirely change the sense of a sentence. An accidental 'not' which is meant to be a 'now' makes all the difference: 'he is not doing well in foster care'. Remember always to apply your brain as well as the spell check – this did not happen when a letter was sent to Great Hormone Street Hospital.

9. Read, redraft and re-read

When you have finished writing your document, put it aside for a while before re-reading it. If you re-read it straight away, you cannot see it with a fresh eye and will miss mistakes, as you know what it is supposed to say. Make sure that you are happy with every single word of your statement – you have to answer to it in the witness box.

Always print off a copy of your statement rather than just reading it on screen – it is surprising how different things look on the printed page. Is it too long or too short? Is it repetitive? Is it clear? The suggested statement checklist in Appendix 1 may help.

Re-read your statement several times, considering it from the perspective of the others who will read it. Ask yourself whether your lawyer will be happy that you have covered all the necessary ground. What will the parents and their solicitors light upon? Where will the child's representatives find fault? Above all, does the statement give the court the information it needs to make the right decision?

10. Ask someone else to check your statement

It is always useful to have someone else's view of your statement. A colleague in your team but not involved in the case can give a fresh perspective and tell you whether you have explained the situation clearly enough to someone who, like the court, does not know the family.

You need constructive criticism – it is no use to you to be told that your work is brilliant – there is always room for improvement. It is far better to be challenged by, and receive helpful suggestions from, someone 'on your side' than to be lulled into a false sense of security only to be put through the mill by the other parties.

Naturally, your lawyer should check your statement before it is submitted. His workload is probably as heavy as yours, so he needs to receive your statement well before the deadline to review it properly. He reads it from a lawyer's perspective, anticipating likely challenges, and may suggest changes or additions. However, it remains your statement, not the lawyer's, so do not accept any changes you do not agree with.

Email allows drafts to be circulated quickly, but first make sure that there is sufficient security on your system to allow such confidential information to be sent safely and always follow any protocols set by your authority. Statements can be amended on screen and returned to sender but if you do allow someone to do this, be absolutely sure that you know what changes they have made – it is possible to track changes to documents – or you could be surprised by the contents of your own statement. Ultimately you have to sign a hard copy. Be certain that the copy you sign is the final and approved version with all amendments incorporated and all corrections made. It is surprisingly easy to get this wrong. One legal firm failed to mark successive drafts of a contract and the client ended up signing the wrong draft, which omitted an important clause. This proved to be an expensive mistake.

Never, ever put your signature to a statement without taking the time to re-read it, line by line.

QUESTIONS FOR REFLECTION:

• What are your strengths and weaknesses in writing?

• How can you address the aspects you find difficult?

Chapter 7

Negotiations and Settlements

Negotiations

From the moment proceedings are issued, discussions start. All the parties, via their lawyers, negotiate through correspondence and phone calls, trying to achieve their objectives or improve their position for court. These negotiations continue right up to the court door.

Social workers often feel uncomfortable about this process; it feels like horse trading, haggling and doing a deal over a child's life. You would not have applied for a care order if you did not think it was the right thing, so why would you change your mind? Remember no one can force you to compromise or accept a settlement against your will. It is open to the local authority to refuse to bend one inch and to insist that the court hears the case in full and makes the decision. However, that may not always be the most productive approach.

In fact there are good reasons for negotiations. Sometimes, an original suggestion is made which you have not considered before. In other cases, a way forward is found which was simply not possible previously because one of the other parties had to move first – for example, the child's mother finally admits that all is not rosy and she needs help. Sometimes strategies and tactics for the case change with time – you might need to try a different service or approach which might work, or if it doesn't, at least you can tell the court you tried. The evidence might just not hold up as you anticipated, and you might have to be realistic and settle for half a loaf instead of none. All kinds of developments can affect how the case proceeds and, together with your lawyer, you need to play your hand to achieve the best realistic outcome for the child.

Why cases settle at court

Even now, in spite of the fact that everyone's position is put in writing early on and despite months of correspondence, sometimes a settlement is reached at the very last minute, even on the day of the final hearing. In fact, most cases reach agreement at least on the threshold criteria before final hearing. Often, parents who have been fighting tooth and nail throughout suddenly cave in when they get to court. Why?

- Suddenly it is real – seeing everyone at court, knowing the judge is there, somehow it all becomes too overwhelming.

- Maybe they knew in their heart of hearts all along but could not face reality until they had no choice.

- All the evidence, including the Guardian's report, is now in and there is no more hope of one last report changing everything.

- The barrister is giving the same advice as their solicitor has, so finally they have no choice but to accept it.

- The idea of all the evidence about their failings being rehearsed in court is just too much.

What are negotiations about?

The court only wants to hear matters really in dispute – that is its job. The parties are expected to narrow the issues in dispute as far as possible. If agreement can be reached on some or all of the issues, it can be presented to court for approval. This is not just a rubber stamping exercise and the court can reject a proposed agreement, insisting on hearing the matter in full instead. However, if the court is happy that the agreement is a sensible one, the case can be resolved quickly without the need to hear evidence. This makes the hearing much less painful for all concerned. The child gets the order he needs more quickly and can be told that everyone agreed it was the right thing for him.

The question is how to get to that agreed position. One possibility is that the parents simply give in and accept everything you say. However, they also wish to achieve something in these proceedings and there may have to be a little give and take to get to the goal of a sensible agreement. The objective in negotiations is to reach a 'win/win' position so everyone can leave court satisfied and with their heads held high. That takes clear thinking and careful planning.

Before entering into any discussions, you need to know:

- your ideal outcome
- your realistic expected outcome
- the other parties' objectives and likely negotiation points
- what you are prepared to negotiate on
- what you are not prepared to negotiate on

- your bottom line, below which you will not go
- how much authority you have to compromise the case (when do you need to contact your senior, and do you know where to contact her on the day?).

This thinking needs to be done in advance and in conjunction with your legal team. If you leave it until the day itself and all proposals come as a complete surprise, you are unlikely to be able to think sufficiently quickly on your feet and may find yourself railroaded into an agreement which, on reflection, is not the best outcome. Imagine how much pressure you could be under if the parents and Guardian, through their articulate and forceful barristers, put forward a proposal which could save five days of court time and avoid the need for you or anyone else to give evidence. The temptation to agree could be irresistible.

Discussions at court sometimes proceed like shuttle diplomacy, the parties each ensconced in separate rooms and people going to and fro with proposals. Make sure you are fully involved in discussions – do not let your advocate go off without you to discuss matters with the other parties unless it is specified as an advocates' meeting only. Sometimes Guardians are present in discussions while social workers are excluded – why should you accept that? Ensure that your lawyer knows that he is not authorised to make any proposals or agree to any compromises without your specific instructions.

If you are present during discussions, remember that agreement may not be reached and you may still end up in court, so be careful not to say anything you might regret, or to give away any weaknesses in your case which could be thrown back at you in cross-examination. Neither should you agree to anything without discussing it in private with your lawyer first. If you need to ask any questions, want to make any suggestions or to take advice, withdraw to discuss matters with your lawyer and make sure you are out of earshot of the other parties before you start talking.

Obviously, the precise details of negotiations depend on the details of the case. The strength of each party's bargaining position depends on the evidence, and the Guardian's position is very influential too. Some possibilities are illustrated in the following scenarios. Put yourself in the shoes of the parents' advocate. What would you ideally like to achieve? What can you realistically salvage for your client? What can you offer to make a 'deal' more attractive to the local authority? How can you best play your hand?

Scenario 7.1: Is an ICO necessary?

The local authority applies for an interim care order in respect of Lottie who is already in foster care. Her mother Millie accepts that Lottie should remain in foster care until the final hearing.

What does Millie's solicitor want to achieve? He wants to:

- avoid the court hearing too much evidence adverse to his client
- portray his client as fully co-operative and sensible
- avoid an interim care order which would give the local authority the upper hand at an early stage.

His ideal is to achieve an adjournment without an interim care order. What, then, will Millie's solicitor do outside court? He will:

- stress that Lottie will remain in foster care, achieving the local authority's main objective without an order
- emphasise Millie's full co-operation
- remind the local authority that there has been no problem with voluntary foster care and the local authority has been content with that until now
- stress that Lottie will be under the protection of the court proceedings throughout – the case can always be brought back to court on short notice if necessary
- remind the local authority of the 'no order' principle and the doctrine of proportionality under the Human Rights Act 1998
- imply that the local authority will lose face when it applies for an interim order and is unsuccessful
- remind the local authority that if Millie fails to co-operate, the local authority will have an unanswerable case next time
- offer a written agreement signed by Millie which can be filed at court
- as a fall-back position, if he cannot avoid a hearing, limit it to submissions on the 'no order' principle and avoid any evidence being heard.

What does the local authority need to be prepared for and to say in response?

Obviously it must be very clear why it wants an interim care order in spite of Millie's co-operation and Lottie's accommodation in foster care.

If it cannot give a good reason for an order it will win neither the negotiations nor the court application.

A tightly drawn written agreement might be a good solution for all concerned at this stage, provided the local authority is clear exactly what needs to be included in such an agreement, which must be drawn up unambiguously. In this case, the parties may spend a couple of hours outside court drafting an agreement to present to the court. The court does not then need to hear any evidence provided it is happy that Lottie is adequately protected in the interim.

So the social worker needs to be very clear about the following before going to court:

- exactly why an interim care order is needed
- whether a written agreement could be enough
- precisely what terms should be included in any written agreement
- who has the authority to compromise the application – the social worker or a more senior officer?

Scenario 7.2: Interim negotiations

Nigella is in foster care under an interim care order. Her mother Odette unsuccessfully contested the first hearing and nothing has changed since. Odette wants Nigella home. Contact is currently twice a week for 1½ hours at the family centre.

What is Odette's solicitor likely to do?

Odette is entitled to contest every interim care order, but the court has discretion to limit the evidence to matters which have changed since the last hearing. Odette's solicitor advises her that her chances of persuading the court to change its mind at this stage are effectively non-existent, so it is best to accept an interim care order for now and concentrate on securing Nigella's return in the long term. Odette can reject this advice and instruct her solicitor to oppose again and, if so, he must follow her instructions. However, assuming she is realistic, what is the fall-back position? If Nigella cannot come home in the interim, the obvious next step is to seek more contact.

His ideal is a programme of phased increases in contact, leading ultimately to rehabilitation, starting with more and longer visits, building towards trips out, then contact at home and so on. Realistically, he knows it is unlikely that he will secure the whole programme in one go, so he might settle for some increase at this stage, and seek more next time. If the local authority does not agree, he can seek a defined contact order, so the social worker could attend court for an interim care hearing and find herself faced instead with an interim contact dispute.

To be prepared for this, she needs to have information about the contact visits to date – has Odette attended regularly? What is the quality of contact? How does Nigella react before, during and after contact? Never go to an interim hearing, even one you expect to be agreed, without being aware of the current situation and having spoken to the contact superviser and foster carer.

In discussions about contact, the worker needs to be able to say why she chose the current level in the first place – who or what is it for? If she cannot explain this, she cannot counter Odette's request for longer or more frequent contact. Courts are usually deeply unimpressed by resource-led answers. 'That's all the family centre could provide' is not a good reason to determine how often Nigella sees her mother. If the family centre is not available more frequently, the riposte is likely to be that there are other possible venues, such as the foster home, Odette's home or McDonalds.

Sometimes it can be a good strategy to call someone's bluff. Of course this is out of the question if Odette poses a real danger to Nigella, but sometimes it can be worth going along with the parent's request. If contact is offered, say, five days a week, at different times of day, sometimes early in the morning, sometimes at mealtimes, then Odette's commitment and her relationship with Nigella are really tested out. Either it works, in which case all well and good, or it fails, providing clear evidence for the court. Either way, the local authority shows itself to be accommodating Odette's wishes and trying its best to make things work.

If, on the other hand, contact continues at the current level and is of reasonable quality, the evidence remains unclear. At the final hearing Odette's lawyers can emphasise the positives and argue that contact shows that Nigella can come home. The local authority counters that a couple of sessions of contact a week is very different from full-time care, but this situation is of the authority's own making and the evidence of contact does not demonstrate why Nigella cannot return home.

Sometimes requests are made for a change of social worker – perhaps on grounds of gender (a teenage boy wants a male worker), or racial origin (a black family want a black worker) or personality (the family claim not to get on with the particular social worker). There may of course be good reasons why such requests cannot be granted, perhaps no black workers are available, or the child already has a strong relationship with the allocated worker, but it is always worth considering carefully. Changing a worker does not imply acceptance of any criticisms and that can be clearly spelled out. Particularly where the request is made simply because the family dislike the allocated worker, there seems to be almost a reflex response to deny the request because parents cannot dictate who is allocated to a case. It is worth reflecting on this for a moment. We have all met people who, perhaps for no apparent reason at all, we do not warm to. Imagine being expected to discuss the most intimate aspects of your life with such a person – would you not ask for a change of worker, and resent it if your request were denied?

A change of worker sometimes works wonders – a productive relationship is established, progress is achieved. Sometimes the parents characterise the first worker as the 'baddie' and put all their resentment and bitterness at the situation onto her, allowing them to move on and work constructively with someone else.

Other parents are unable to work with anyone and soon complain about the next person. But if a change of worker is tried, by the time of the final hearing the local authority has clear evidence of its good faith and flexibility as well as demonstrating that the problem lies with the parents, not the authority.

Scenario 7.3: Debating the final care plan

Peter is five. By the time of the final hearing the evidence shows that his mother Queenie cannot care for him full time. However, Queenie has been committed to contact throughout and everyone agrees that there is a positive relationship between Peter and his mother. Because of his age, the local authority plans to place Peter for adoption. It applies for a care order and a placement order, judging a permanent placement to be more important for Peter than continued contact.

Queenie's solicitor has advised her that the local authority's case is strong and it is hopeless to try to contest the care order. It may even be counter-productive to do so, as this would show her as lacking insight, she would have to go through days of hearing damning evidence and could end up with stronger findings against her than if she concedes the care order. If the care order is a lost cause, what then is her solicitor's approach?

- His ideal objective is to secure a change in the care plan, for example, to long-term fostering with ongoing contact rather than adoption.

- He can tell the local authority that his client could accept a care order, saving everyone time and trouble, but in return needs some concessions on contact.

- His fall-back position may be to accept adoption as a care plan, but to seek a contact order with the placement order.

- If he cannot secure a contact order compelling the local authority to place with ongoing contact, he might instead seek a commitment in the care plan to try at least for a specified period to find adopters who accept ongoing contact.

The local authority should already have considered these possibilities in case planning. Arguments about the respective merits of long-term fostering and adoption as well as the newer option of Special Guardianship should have been rehearsed and resolved long since as should the issue of post-adoption contact. The court will not accept a simple proposition that it is not possible to find adopters to accept 'open' adoption; where contact is beneficial for the child, evidence should show that this option has been properly explored before being rejected as impracticable. The court can, of course, make an order for contact against the local authority's wishes even if that effectively means changing the care plan.

Evidence of matters such as the likelihood of placement and feasibility of ongoing direct contact in an adoptive placement should be given by the appropriate witness, probably a member of the adoption team rather than the key social worker.

Always beware of the danger of contact being seen as a 'consolation prize' for the parent who is losing a child. Also beware of the temptation to settle to avoid immediate difficulties, only to set up problems for the future.

Scenario 7.4: Rehabilitation

Care proceedings are coming to a conclusion with Roger recently placed at home with his father, Sam. Everyone agrees that rehabilitation is the right plan. To date, all looks good and there is a co-operative working relationship between Sam and the social worker.

Everyone is keen to avoid conflict and no one wants the court process to jeopardise the positive situation. Sam's solicitor can use that as a bargaining point to urge the local authority to take the least adversarial line possible.

Sam's solicitor argues:

- The case should be concluded with no order at all. He cites the 'no order' principle in the Children Act and the proportionality principle under the Human Rights Act. He wants to avoid any findings adverse to his client.

- His fall-back position is to seek an adjournment, if necessary with an interim supervision order, so that the placement can be tested with the proceedings continuing for a while, leading eventually to no order. The target time limit of 40 weeks for care proceedings is not statutory and sometimes the court can and should be persuaded that it is in everybody's best interests to delay the final hearing for a short time.

- If he cannot secure an adjournment, he argues for supervision order, rather than a care order, relying on a string of case law authorities which indicate that where a child is placed at home the presumption is in favour of the least Draconian order, namely a supervision order.

The local authority should be very clear what order, if any, is required, when and why. In fact, an adjournment might be best for everybody. If the case has to be concluded before rehabilitation is sufficiently tried and tested, a care order might be the only safe proposal. But there are disadvantages in having a care order over a child placed at home – the local authority would have legal responsibility for Roger, but little actual control. If the rehabilitation works, another court case would later be required to dispose of the care order. If the rehabilitation proves unsuccessful, it might still be necessary to return to court for another order such as a placement order, if adoption is the contingency plan, or an order regulating contact. From the authority's managers' point of view, statistics are another consideration – why have another child under a care order if it is not necessary? Adjourning under interim orders for a few months may enable the right outcome to become clear.

Scenario 7.5: Agreeing the threshold findings

Care proceedings are underway in respect of Tim and Ursula's children. The local authority seek care orders and orders giving leave to refuse contact under s34(4) Children Act 1989, the plan being long term fostering. The local authority's case rests on three main issues:

1. Sexual abuse of the children by Tim, the evidence being the children's disclosures and medical signs 'consistent' with sexual abuse, although Tim was acquitted in the criminal court.

2. Physical abuse in the form of excessive chastisement including beating the children with a stick.

3. Emotional abuse, especially both parents' emotional rejection of the children.

Up to the final hearing, the parents contest all three points, strenuously denying sexual abuse, claiming that their punishment of the children was reasonable and consistent with their religious faith and rejecting allegations of emotional abuse.

However, although they deny the allegations, they do not want the children back or to see them again, so hurt and betrayed do they feel. This means that their solicitor can tell the local authority it can have the orders it wants, the witnesses can all go home and everyone can breathe a sigh of relief. What else is there left to argue about?

The local authority needs to consider not just orders, but also the findings on which they are based – the court can only make a care order if the s31 threshold criteria are met. Negotiations in this case therefore turn on whether the findings can be agreed. The temptation to reach agreement is very strong, but in an effort to compromise, the local authority must not allow the findings to be watered down too far. Many of us have seen agreed findings which barely cross the threshold and are so understated as to be nearly meaningless.

Tim and Ursula accept that they have hit the children, although they believe they had Biblical authority for this, and they admit that they have now emotionally rejected the children because of the allegations. They are willing to accept a threshold document recording these concessions. They are absolutely not prepared to sign up to anything mentioning sexual abuse.

Can the local authority accept Tim and Ursula's offer? The local authority team need to consider the strength or otherwise of the evidence and consider the longer term consequences of findings. What if, a couple of years on, Tim and Ursula ask to see the children or have another child? The social worker at that time will no doubt look at the court's findings. She might take a very different decision depending on whether or not there are findings of sexual abuse.

There are implications for the children themselves, including questions of therapy and criminal injuries compensation. The local authority might just have to bite the bullet and insist on the court hearing evidence even though the orders themselves are conceded.

Scenario 7.6: Threshold concessions

Vanessa's case also turns on the issue of findings. She is an 18-year-old mother who had a difficult childhood herself and although she tried to look after baby William accepts she could not manage. She agrees to a care order and placement order, with a view to William's adoption. What, then, can Vanessa's solicitor achieve for her?

The best he can realistically hope for is:

- assurances about ongoing contact (indirect at least)

- input for his client in the adoption process (choice of adopters, meeting adopters, preparing life book/letter/gift)

- mildly worded agreed findings which will do as little damage as possible to Vanessa's prospects of keeping any babies she may have in the future.

- positive comments from the judge about how brave Vanessa is in reaching this difficult decision, putting her child's interests above her own.

Judges often, quite rightly, pay tribute to parents in cases where they concede orders, enabling them to leave court with some dignity even after losing their child. Imagine the contrast to the damning judgment describing every last failure which might have followed a contested hearing in the same case. This is one of the reasons why parents' solicitors must be brutally honest with their clients about their prospects of success should they choose to contest. Imagine how it feels to spend days in court having your life dissected and your every move criticised by one witness after another, followed by a judgment detailing your failings as a parent, on top of the pain of losing your child. Sometimes, therefore, the best service a parent's solicitor can give to his client is to help her recognise reality and to end the proceedings with some self-esteem intact.

Conclusion

Negotiations are an integral part of court proceedings. Be prepared for them. Be clear about your objectives and realistic about your prospects. Be open to suggestions or new ways of thinking, always putting the child's best interests at the heart of your deliberations.

Chapter 8

Procedure

The Protocol

There is no getting away from it – procedure is dull. It seems far from your focus in the case, which is quite properly on the child. However, to serve your child client well, you need to understand the structure of a case and be well prepared for each of the steps to be undertaken.

Since November 2003 the procedure in care proceedings cases has been standardised by the snappily titled 'Protocol for Judicial Case Management in Public Law Children Act Cases', universally known as 'the Protocol'. This was described in its foreword as a 'distillation of best practice'. It introduced the target of 40 weeks for the completion of care proceedings (which by then were taking almost a year), achieved by the introduction of standard procedures and greater judicial control of the proceedings. An eminent group of High Court judges reported in December 2005 on the progress of the Protocol[1] and noted in their report: 'there are still practitioners in all of the child care professions who appear never to have read the Protocol and in particular the best practice documents annexed to it' (p.18). Make sure you are not one of those practitioners; it is essential reading.

The general view is that the Protocol has improved matters overall, but some adjustments to its provisions are expected. At the time of writing, the standard documentation is under review, one complaint about the Protocol being the large amount of paperwork and duplication involved. There may also be changes to the early stages of proceedings, including a possible pre-proceedings protocol, to try to divert matters from court altogether, and an initial court-led conciliation and dispute resolution appointment to try to resolve the

---

1   Judicial Review Team (2005) *Thematic Review of the Protocol for Judicial Case Management in Public Law Children Act Cases.* London: Judicial Communications Office. Accessed on 1/5/07 at http://www.judiciary.gov.uk/publications_media/general/index.htm# family.

case at an early stage. It is important for you to keep up to date with developments in procedure.

Over time we can also expect to see greater use of technology than at present, telephone or video conferencing replacing some court hearings, and greater use of email.

Procedure is perhaps best understood in the context of a sample case.

Scenario 8.1: A non-accidental injury?

Xavier (aged 6 months) is not known to Social Services until the local consultant paediatrician, Dr Yates, contacts social worker Ms Zachary, as he has admitted Xavier to hospital suffering from a subdural haemotoma and numerous finger-type bruise marks to his body. Xavier is in the paediatric intensive care unit. Dr Yates's opinion is that the injuries are probably non-accidental in origin. Xavier's mother Ms Andrews and her partner Mr Barlow explain that while Ms Andrews was changing Xavier on the bed, she turned her back for a moment and he accidentally rolled off the bed onto the floor. Mr Barlow says he heard Ms Andrews scream, he ran upstairs to find Xavier unconscious and called the ambulance immediately. Dr Yates does not find this explanation plausible.

Ms Zachary immediately commences an initial assessment and holds an urgent inter-agency strategy discussion. The legal adviser, Mr Cohen, advises that there are grounds for care proceedings, but no need for an Emergency Protection Order as Xavier is currently safe in hospital. The local authority decides to start care proceedings and to seek an interim care order (ICO).

Stage 1: The application

Ms Zachary, with guidance from Mr Cohen, completes forms C1 (general application form) and C13 (supplement for care proceedings). In the C1 she includes all the necessary basic information including Xavier's full name, sex and date of birth, his parents' details, and the local authority ('LA') details while the C13 is the specific supplement for care proceedings, setting out the grounds and reasons for the proposed action, initial plans and directions sought.

The basis of the case must be clear from these forms, which are the first documents received by the court as well as by the parents and Guardian and their respective solicitors. There are no ongoing proceedings concerning Xavier, so the case starts in the Family Proceedings Court ('FPC').

Ms Zachary and Mr Cohen must immediately set about producing the LA's documents which have to be filed at court and served on the other parties to the proceedings within the next two days. These are the initial assessment (if Xavier's case had been one of planned care proceedings, such as a case of long-term neglect, the full core assessment would already have been done, and should be filed), the initial social work statement and social work chronology. In this case, the LA is also clearly relying on the paediatrician's opinion, so Mr Cohen must ask Dr Yates for a statement.

On receiving the application, the FPC immediately directs the appointment of a Children's Guardian by CAFCASS. Mrs Dunn, the Guardian, must be appointed by day three, and she selects Mr Evans, a solicitor from the Children Panel, to act for Xavier. If there had been a waiting list for Guardians, the court would have appointed the child's solicitor itself.

The FPC also immediately fixes the first hearing, to take place by day six. It issues a Notice of Hearing which is served on the parties along with the application forms. All parties must immediately plan for this hearing, bearing in mind that time is short.

Mrs Dunn must start her enquiries straight away and progress as far as she realistically can before the first hearing, discussing the case with Mr Evans.

Ms Andrews has to find a solicitor who can take her case on. She phones several local Children Panel solicitors before finding that Mr Foster can take the case. He gives her an urgent appointment to fill in the Legal Aid forms, take instructions and give advice on the case so far, including in particular whether or not to accept an ICO. Luckily he is available to attend the first hearing himself – if not, he would have to find an agent or instruct a barrister to cover it for him.

Stage 2: First FPC hearing

All parties attend court with their lawyers, who make submissions to the court for decision on immediate issues including:

- *Party status* Has everyone who is entitled to be a party to the proceedings been served with the papers and should anyone else be a party?

    In our scenario, on further enquiry, it turns out that Xavier's father is not Mr Barlow, but Mr Andrews, who has parental responsibility as he was married to Xavier's mother although they separated before the birth. He automatically has party status, so has to be served immediately with all of the papers.

    Should Mr Barlow be a party as well? The court decides this after hearing submissions from all the other parties. At this stage, his case is the same as Mrs Andrews's, so he may not need to be a party in his own right; he can simply be a witness on her behalf, but the court might allow him be present during the proceedings.

Later in the case Ms Andrews might change her story and accuse Mr Barlow of causing the injuries. If so, he might be joined to the proceedings as a party or as an 'intervenor', a status which allows him to defend himself against those accusations, including hearing the relevant evidence and being represented, but without giving him a role in other aspects of the case.

- *Interim care order* Mrs Andrews does not consent to an ICO and wants to contest the application. Mr Andrews's position is unknown at the moment. The FPC could grant an immediate order, but as Xavier is still in hospital, the court adjourns the application for a contested hearing on another date. This contest could be in the FPC or the Care Centre (County Court) depending on the outcome of the next issue:

- *Transfer* Is the FPC the right court to conduct this case all the way through to final hearing? The decision is one for the court, after hearing submissions from the parties (and subject to possible appeal). In less complicated cases which stay in the FPC throughout, the court gives case management directions at the first hearing. There are concerns that too many cases are transferred and that, as a result, FPCs are losing experience and expertise.

In our scenario, all the parties and the court agree that the case must be transferred up on the grounds of gravity, complexity and likely length of final hearing. Until the unified family court service is fully introduced, this means transferring the case to a different building and different administration. The FPC immediately calls the County Court to arrange an allocation hearing and contested interim care hearing date, which should be by day 11. The parties are usually notified of the date and time of that hearing before they leave the FPC. The FPC then leaves the rest of the case to the Care Centre and limits itself to ordering either Mr Cohen or Mr Evans to prepare and file within the next two days a case synopsis for the County Court. Appendix B to the Protocol sets out what this document should include. Unsurprisingly, it is a brief document, no more than two sides of A4. It identifies the parties, the nature of the case and any particular issues which the County Court needs to address early on – in this case the need for a contested interim hearing is obvious, and the possibility of criminal proceedings might also be flagged up, as the police are investigating the case as possible grievous bodily harm. Mr Cohen is responsible for drafting this document but Ms Zachary makes sure she sees and comments on the draft before it is submitted.

Stage 3: Allocations hearing, directions and interim care hearing

The County Court office allocates one or two case management judges who remain with the case throughout, including the final hearing. Our case is allocated to District Judge (DJ) Gates, who will deal with directions and interim case management, and the Circuit Judge His Honour Judge Howard who will decide major issues including the final hearing.

The DJ hears the allocation hearing by day 11. The Protocol expects contested interim applications to be determined at this hearing but in practice there may not be enough time available to deal with a contest as well as directions.

Interim hearings are not a dress rehearsal for the final hearing. Findings of disputed fact should be rare and the evidence should be restricted to matters essential to establishing a holding position. Nevertheless Mr Foster argues for Mrs Andrews that she must have the opportunity to put her own evidence before the court. Mr Andrews's solicitor, Mr Ingram, points out that his client has only just been notified of the proceedings and needs time to prepare his position, but it is already clear that he is not implicated in the injuries and he says he can care for Xavier, a suggestion opposed by Mrs Andrews. Both solicitors argue human rights points under Article 6 (right to a fair trial) and Article 8 (right to respect for private and family life) and point out that Xavier is still in hospital so there is no pressing need for an urgent decision.

District Judge Gates decides in the circumstances to fix a separate interim care hearing on an early date when more court time is available. He gives directions for statements and an interim care plan to be filed and served in advance. In the meantime, he gets on with case management directions, using the Standard Directions Form, found in Appendix A/1 to the Protocol.

At this early stage the dates are set for significant hearings. These are the Case Management Conference ('CMC'), at any time between days 15 and 60, the Pre-Hearing Review ('PHR'), between 2 and 8 weeks before the final hearing, and the final hearing itself, within the 40 weeks maximum timescale. Before coming to court, therefore, Mr Cohen has found out availability details of all known witnesses, Dr Yates included, so the final hearing is fixed on a convenient date. At this early stage, some of the witnesses and issues have not yet been identified, so parties can do little more than make an educated guess at how many days the final hearing will take, and the time estimate may need to be revised later.

Mr Cohen and Ms Zachary have discussed in advance what work needs to be done on the case and how long it will take, so that Mr Cohen can make submissions to DJ Gates on when the local authority evidence can be filed. This work includes completing the core assessment, including all family members, as well as considering extended family as possible carers and holding a family group conference. Given Xavier's young age, adoption is a possible final care plan, and Ms Zachary must consider twin tracking, remembering that all procedures have to be completed within the tight timescale – if adoption ultimately becomes the care plan proposed to the court, Ms Zachary must fit in consideration of Xavier's case by the Best Interests Panel and submit a placement order application to be heard alongside the final care application.

The LA team need to consider which other witnesses to approach for statements or information, such as the paramedics who took Xavier to hospital, Xavier's health visitor and GP as well as any other Social Services staff, such as contact supervisors. As the case goes on, Ms Zachary must keep Mr Cohen informed of other professionals involved in Xavier's life, so that he can consider any evidential implications.

Together, they need to consider whether there are other documents in Social Services' possession which should be disclosed, or whether to approach other agencies for more information, such as requesting Xavier's nursing notes; these might include matters of interest beyond medical information such as frequency of family visits and observations of parent/child interactions. Notes or recordings of any police interviews with Mrs Andrews or Mr Barlow might be important.

The DJ fixes a timetable not just for hearings but also for evidence and documents to be filed and served by each party. Usually, one party follows another so, for example, the LA files its final evidence first, the parents following two or three weeks later, and the Guardian last, a week or so after that. If Ms Zachary is late with her final evidence, the whole timetable is put out and other parties run out of time to put their case. The structure of the directions fixed by DJ Gates depends on all parties complying with the deadlines.

The parties use the Case Management Checklist (Appendix A3 to the Protocol) to prepare for the hearing. This extensive list of issues is a helpful aide-mémoire for consideration at every stage of the case, but is not filed at court.

Throughout, everyone should bear in mind whether anyone involved – parties, witnesses or advocates – has any special needs. Sometimes interpreters are needed (for spoken or signed languages); they are available but are in short supply, so advance planning is needed. Some court buildings (usually the newer ones) have better facilities for wheelchair users than others, so a transfer to a different court might be in order. If someone needs to lip-read, seating arrangements in court may need to be changed, which again may influence the choice of venue. Cultural issues need to be considered, such as bearing in mind relevant Holy Days when fixing hearing dates. Flexibility is usually possible to cater for any particular features of a case but it requires someone to think of it and the social worker, being more aware of equal opportunities issues than most in the court arena, is quite likely to be the person to do so. She must feel confident to raise the issue, and not assume that someone else will, or that it cannot be a valid point because no one else has mentioned it.

Advance planning is also required to ensure any technology required is available on the day. Courts are increasingly well equipped, but there is likely to be only one TV link room available, for example, so it must be booked in advance. If a video is to be shown or a tape played in the hearing, the equipment must be in the court room on the day. Thinking ahead is essential and the earlier these matters are raised, the better.

In terms of case preparation too, each case is different and directions are needed to suit the case in question. In Xavier's case, the question of medical evidence is bound to be raised, the opinion of a single treating paediatrician being unlikely to go unchallenged. Expert evidence is often considered at the CMC but where it is clearly an issue (as in our scenario) the earlier it is addressed the better, so it should be raised at the first County Court hearing.

Other considerations include whether there should be a split hearing (again a likely issue in our scenario), a s38(6) direction for a particular assessment, perhaps including a residential assessment, or directions to cater for twin tracking and consolidated applications under the Adoption and Children Act 2002.

Expert evidence

In Xavier's case applications will inevitably be made for more medical evidence from experts who are not involved in Xavier's treatment, but instructed specifically for the court proceedings. These will probably include a second paediatric opinion, commenting on Dr Yates's views, and specialists from other fields such as a paediatric radiologist. Appendix C to the Protocol gives detailed guidance on instructing experts.

WHEN AND WHY ARE EXPERTS INSTRUCTED?

Experts should only be instructed to give an opinion on a question which is not within the court's skill and experience and which is relevant and necessary for the court's decision. In cases with medical or psychiatric elements, the need for an expert may be clear, but this is less so for a general 'family assessment'. Sometimes experts such as psychologists seem to be instructed simply to validate social work opinion. Some of these psychologists carry out their assessments in a single appointment. Parent clients often ask their solicitors how anyone can claim to know them in an hour and a half – you might agree that is a fair question. When they arrive, their reports may seem to regurgitate large chunks of the social worker's statement.

This situation has come about because of lack of confidence in social work professionalism – indeed the Judicial Review Team in its report on the Protocol[2] noted that one of the issues raised by their respondents was that 'the level of skill and expertise being provided by available social care professionals in particular when undertaking vital family assessments and in care planning is not of a sufficiently high standard'(p. 17). Part of the drive for increasing professionalism in social work is aimed at addressing these perceptions and their underlying cause. You can play your part in improving your profession's reputation by the quality of your work and its presentation.

In fact, validation of a social work assessment is not a proper use of experts. The Protocol demands that particular justification should be given before the court allows an expert assessment on a subject within the expertise of Social Services and/or the Guardian. You and your legal team should challenge any application for such an assessment.

There is also a danger that experts are instructed in an effort to find a solution where it is simply unrealistic to expect one. In one case, doubtless not unique, social workers assessed the case thoroughly, found it very complex and struggled to reach an ideal care plan for the children. The Guardian felt the same way. The parties all decided to seek advice from a nationally renowned centre and the judge, acknowledging that the case was difficult, agreed. When the report finally arrived, everyone read it with bated breath waiting for the oracle to pronounce the answer. Several thousand pounds and several months' wait were rewarded with a conclusion which effectively said 'isn't this hard?' and listed the options the parties already knew they had. Sometimes there is no simple answer and no expert in the world can give you one.

The time involved in obtaining an expert opinion should be weighed in the balance with the realistic anticipated benefits of the opinion. The Judicial Review Team noted 'It remains a stark fact that the time that is taken to identify key issues, find and select an expert and receive their advice is the single greatest driver of delay in the determination of most care cases' (p. 10).

You do not have to agree to an expert being instructed. If another party seeks one and you do not believe it to be necessary, instruct your lawyer to oppose the application.

2   Judicial Review Team (2005) *Thematic Review of the Protocol for Judicial Case Management in Public Law Children Act Cases.* London: Judicial Communications Office. Accessed on 19/1/07 at http://www.judiciary.gov.uk/publications_media/general/index.htm# family.

HOW ARE EXPERTS CHOSEN?

It usually takes considerable time and innumerable phone calls to find an expert with appropriate competence and experience, who is available within a suitable timescale and can come to court for the final hearing. There is such great demand and such limited supply in some fields that if an expert is free, one is left wondering why – what is wrong with him? At present there are no accreditation or quality control schemes, although this issue is under active consideration, so experts become known simply by reputation.

Social workers should be fully involved in deciding which expert should be selected. Ask to see a full CV – it is not just a question of qualification in a specific discipline, but specialisation within that field. Being an expert witness is a skill in itself – make sure the person proposed has experience in legal proceedings. What is his reputation? Do you know anyone who has seen his work – are his reports good and is he effective in court? Some experts are fine on paper, but unimpressive in oral evidence. How does he conduct his assessments – does he expect the family to go to his consulting rooms in Harley Street or does he come to them? How many sessions of what length does he propose? Be assertive in seeking information to help you decide on the right response to the application.

Other factors such as gender are relevant – a male psychiatrist, however eminent, may not be the right person to assess a sexually abused teenage girl. Racial and cultural factors may also be important, and personality can be a factor. One psychiatrist was blunt to the point of cruelty, including in his report a description of an adolescent who may indeed have been overweight and spotty but who did not need to read that in a report.

WHAT COURT ORDERS ARE NEEDED?

The court decides whether an expert should be instructed or not and only gives permission if provided with full details to justify the application. Directions specify who is to take responsibility for instructing the expert, distributing the report, arranging the expert's attendance at court and paying his fees. If permission is granted, the expert receives a full copy of the bundle of documents filed at court, and the solicitor instructing him must ensure it is kept up to date. The expert does not have the right to examine the child unless the court gives him specific permission to do so, but it is always open to a competent child to refuse an examination or assessment.

LETTER OF INSTRUCTION

The instruction letter is an important document and guidance appears in Appendix C to the Protocol. The letter should be drafted by a lawyer, not a social worker. However, it is very important that the social worker sees the draft and contributes to it, especially in formulating the precise questions to be asked. Appendix C says that these should be clear, focused and direct and kept to a manageable number. That they should be drafted in a neutral way may sound obvious, but nevertheless one solicitor wrote to a psychiatrist saying 'we know you're not Mystic Meg but please can you look into your crystal ball and tell the court that Mrs X will recover soon and be able to look after her daughter'! The draft letter is circulated to the other parties and, ideally, an agreed version is arrived at, but in default the court decides.

ARE EXPERTS' REPORTS DISCLOSED?

Once permission is given for an expert to be instructed, the report must be disclosed come what may. In our case, if Mr Foster on Mrs Andrews's behalf instructs an expert, he has no choice but to file and serve the report when it arrives, even if it completely contradicts his client's case, confirming that the injuries are non-accidental and that her explanation is implausible.

WHEN ARE EXPERTS' MEETINGS HELD?

Some cases involve more than one expert from the same or related disciplines. Xavier's case will involve at least the hospital paediatrician, an independent expert paediatrician and a paediatric radiologist. It makes sense that, before the hearing, the experts put their heads together and see where they agree and disagree. An experts' discussion or meeting is organised and chaired by the child's solicitor, using a list of questions circulated in advance to all parties, and results in a Statement of Agreement and Disagreement submitted to the court and the parties. The court can then focus on the areas of dispute.

DO EXPERTS COME TO COURT TO GIVE EVIDENCE?

Unless their evidence is accepted by all parties and no one wants to cross-examine, expert witnesses attend court. Where there is more than one expert, if possible they all come to court on the same day and are allowed to remain in court to hear each other's evidence.

WHO PAYS?

Expert witnesses do not come cheap; four-figure sums are the norm. The court decides who pays for the report, and often the cost is shared between the parties, regardless of who raised the suggestion. Parents and children's solicitors have to secure funding from the Legal Services Commission and the local authority has to find the money somewhere in its budget – no mean feat in either case. As soon as anyone suggests instructing an expert you should alert the relevant budget holder immediately, and make sure you do not agree to anything without the decision-maker's permission. The instructions to the expert must include details of the funding arrangements. If your department has imposed an upper limit, make sure this is clearly set out in the letter.

Split hearings

In care proceedings, the court's decision essentially boils down to two questions:

1.   Are the threshold criteria met?

If, and only if, the answer is 'yes' then:

2.   What order, if any, should be made?

The idea has therefore evolved that, in appropriate cases, the two questions can be considered separately. This makes sense where the case turns on a single stark issue of fact and Xavier's case might be one such case. The first issue is a factual one – was his injury simply an accident or was it non-accidental, be it deliberate abuse or through unduly rough handling and if so, by whom? If it was a simple accident, the court does not need to progress to question 2 – the threshold has not been crossed, there is no question of an order and everyone can go home and live happily ever after. If, on the other hand, the court decides that his injuries were non-accidental, everyone must go on to consider question 2 in the light of the court's findings.

Imagine how differently you would proceed in your assessments for stage 2 if the court decided that:

(a)   Mr Barlow shook Xavier violently, he has a vicious temper and has assaulted Mrs Andrews who lives in fear of him.

Or:

(b)   Mrs Andrews, tired and under stress, shook Xavier (a very colicky baby) just to make him stop crying, not meaning to hurt him.

The issue of how Xavier came by his injuries is therefore considered by the court in one hearing, often known as a 'fact finding' or 'causation' hearing. Assessments then proceed on the basis of those findings, and some time later a second hearing (sometimes rather unfortunately known as a 'disposal' hearing) decides what order, if any, should be made.

In Xavier's case, the important witnesses in the first hearing are the medical experts, together with witnesses of fact such as the paramedics who were first on the scene, as well as Mrs Andrews and Mr Barlow, both of whom are expected to give their account of events leading to the injury. The social worker and Guardian have a limited role at the first stage; they come into their own for the second stage of assessments and recommendations based on the court's findings of fact.

Stage 4: Case management conference

The case management conference (CMC) takes place between 15 and 60 days into the proceedings. Before the hearing, all parties must file whatever documents the DJ ordered at the Allocations hearing. The local authority files first, five days before the CMC, followed three days later by the other parties.

Ms Zachary must update her social work chronology and, assuming there has not been a causation hearing, Mr Cohen must file the Schedule of Findings of Fact the LA asks the court to make. This is an important document as it sets out the factual basis for the LA's contention that the threshold is crossed. Although drafting this document is clearly the lawyer's responsibility, Ms Zachary should contribute to its preparation. In our scenario, the factual issues are clear and limited in number, but in other cases the Schedule could be a long and detailed document, for example in neglect cases where the local authority needs to seek findings about specific incidents and chronic problems.

The local authority must also complete a Case Management Questionnaire (Appendix A/2 to the Protocol) which highlights issues of evidence, witnesses and identifies directions sought. It is also Mr Cohen's job to prepare the court bundle, following a prescribed format. The bundle is essentially an indexed and paginated lever arch file (several in some cases) containing all of the applications, orders, statements and reports. The other parties prepare their own copy from the index. Ms Zachary should have a full bundle of papers and keep it up to date when new documents come in.

The other parties must also file a Case Management Questionnaire and a position statement setting out what is and is not agreed. This is an important document which helps to define exactly which questions fall to be decided by the court.

Before the CMC the advocates who will conduct the final hearing should meet, usually without clients being present, to put their heads together and draw up for the court a Schedule of Issues. This summarises the case, the questions for the court at the CMC, timetable of outstanding legal and social work steps and looks ahead to the PHR and final hearing, including an updated time estimate.

At the CMC the dates for the PHR and final hearing are fixed or confirmed, and any further directions given to make sure that the final hearing will be effective.

There could be a long gap between the CMC and PHR. All parties have a responsibility to make sure that the case stays on track, that directions are complied with and evidence filed on time. Even if no other hearings have been anticipated, it is always possible to ask the court for another directions hearing if need be and it is far better to address delays, problems or changes in circumstances swiftly than to leave them and hope they will go away.

Stage 5: Pre-hearing review

The pre-hearing review (PHR) is at a late stage in the case, and is held if necessary to make sure all is ready to proceed to trial. By this stage most, if not all, of the final evidence should have been submitted, so it should be quite clear where all parties stand. There is another advocates' discussion or, if necessary, a meeting in the week before the PHR to narrow issues and identify outstanding questions for the court. The advocates work through the checklist in Appendix A/5 to the Protocol, ensuring that evidence has been filed as expected, identifying which witnesses are required to attend court, checking that any special facilities or measures required are in place, and agreeing on their time estimate for the final hearing. Between them, they draw up a Summary of Issues for the case, a list of questions for the PHR, a witness template and decide on the revised time estimate for the final hearing, plus any necessary directions.

The PHR is conducted by the judge who will conduct the final hearing, in our case His Honour Judge Howard.

Stage 6: Final hearing

This is the culmination of all the effort and paperwork. By this stage, the court bundle probably stretches over several hundred pages of statements and reports. His Honour Judge Howard has already assiduously read and thoroughly absorbed all the paperwork before setting foot in court. The parties continue to conduct negotiations outside court until the last moment.

How a contested hearing works

The parties (Ms Zachary included) and their advocates remain in court throughout the hearing. Others, including witnesses, are excluded unless the judge decides otherwise. Everyone rises when Judge Howard enters the room. The advocates bow – technically not to the judge but to the Royal Crest behind his seat. Once the judge is seated, everyone sits except the local authority's advocate, Mr Cohen, who remains on his feet to open the case. In a criminal trial the jury know nothing about the case they are about to hear, so the opening is quite lengthy, to give them all the information they need. In our care proceedings case, Judge Howard already knows exactly what the case is about and what he has to decide. If Mr Cohen tries to address the judge like a jury he will be asked to move on. His opening is therefore brief, identifying the people in court, briefly outlining the matters in dispute, telling the judge which witnesses he will hear and in what order, and very little else. The hearing moves very quickly to the witnesses' evidence.

As the applicant, the local authority presents its case first, calling its witnesses one after the other with Mr Cohen aiming to start and finish with strong witnesses. Ms Zachary, the key worker in the case, is likely to be called first followed by the other local authority witnesses. However some witnesses, particularly experts, may be called out of turn if they have only limited availability.

When Ms Zachary steps into the witness box, she first takes the oath or the affirmation. These promises to tell the truth are of equal value, the only difference being that the oath has a religious basis, whereas the affirmation does not. They signal the formal start of evidence, and anything untrue said thereafter could give rise to a perjury charge. It is a significant moment and everyone else in court should remain silent while the oath is taken. Remember this when you are present when someone else takes the oath.

A witness who elects to take the oath is asked to take the New Testament or other appropriate religious book in her right hand and to read aloud the words on the card held up by the court usher. If you know that a witness cannot read, it is thoughtful to tip the usher off in advance so she can ask that witness to repeat the words after her, rather than read them from the card – it saves embarrassment for all concerned.

The form of oath for Christians is: 'I swear by Almighty God that the evidence I shall give shall be the truth, the whole truth and nothing but the truth.' Appropriate wordings and religious books are available for members of other faiths. The affirmation is: 'I solemnly, sincerely and truly declare and affirm that the evidence I shall give shall be the truth, the whole truth and nothing but the truth.'

After the oath comes Ms Zachary's 'evidence in chief' when she responds to questions from Mr Cohen, her own advocate. He is only allowed to ask open questions and cannot lead his own witness. In criminal trials, examination in chief is a lengthy stage as the witness has to go through her evidence from start to finish. In care proceedings, this is not necessary as everything is already in writing and the judge does not need or want it all to be repeated. All Ms Zachary has to do is to confirm that the contents of all her statements are true to the best of her knowledge and belief, and this has the same effect as if she had recounted every detail on oath. If there are any errors in her statements, this is the time for her to correct them.

Mr Cohen may then ask Ms Zachary to tell the judge of any developments since her last statement and comment on the Guardian's report, but the judge will become impatient if he asks much more. Very quickly, therefore, the next stage, 'cross-examination', is reached. Mrs Zachary is asked questions by the other parties' representatives, each in turn, with Mr Evans having the last turn on Xavier's behalf.

The final stage is 're-examination', when Mr Cohen has the opportunity to ask Ms Zachary further questions, but he can only ask about matters raised in cross-examination – it is not a chance for him to address issues he forgot earlier. Re-examination is an opportunity to clarify anything left unclear and repair any damage done by cross-examination and usually consists of no more than a couple of questions, if any.

Judge Howard can ask any questions he likes whenever he likes. If he wishes, he can take over the questioning and have a debate with the witness. Some judges are very interventionist, others say nothing at all – it depends on personal style. Magistrates tend to intervene less than judges, and usually wait until all the advocates have finished before asking any questions.

When everyone has finished their questions, the judge will give Ms Zachary permission to resume her seat and listen to the rest of the evidence. Other witnesses need to be released by the judge if they want to leave the court building when they have finished their evidence.

Each local authority witness goes through the same process in turn. When they have all given evidence, the local authority's case is concluded and the other parties present their cases, each calling their witnesses. Mrs Andrews's case will probably come next, followed by her ex-husband, and any other parties (such as grandparents putting themselves forward as carers). The child's case always goes last and the final witness is Mrs Dunn, the Guardian.

When all the evidence is concluded the advocates make their submissions to the judge. These are usually put in writing, but may be supplemented by oral submissions. Each highlights all the evidence in his client's favour while explaining away adverse evidence, and puts his arguments on relevant statute and case law.

All that is left then is the judgment, in which Judge Howard gives his decision and reasons. He may deliver this immediately, or he may reserve his judgment to allow time for further consideration. All parties might be asked to attend to hear his reserved judgment or he may hand it down in writing. In his judgment he is likely not only to announce his findings of fact but also comment on what he made of the witnesses – who impressed him, who did not. The following chapters should help you to be one of the impressive witnesses.

QUESTIONS FOR REFLECTION

- How can you avoid missing deadlines for your evidence?
- What can you do to ensure the case runs smoothly?

Chapter 9

Preparing for Court

Some – perhaps all – of this chapter may read like an egg-sucking manual for grandmothers. But sometimes the obvious has to be stated, and every single one of these points has been missed by someone at some time.

Preparing your case

Paperwork

Re-read your statement(s). By the time of the final hearing, your initial statement could be nine months old so you need to refresh your memory. Knowing exactly what you said and where you said it will help you enormously in the witness box. A consultant psychologist in the High Court was once referred to a particular paragraph in her own report and seemed almost surprised by what she had written! Clearly she had not re-read the document since she had written it several months earlier. Coupled with the fact that she repeatedly got the child's name wrong, her credibility was severely dented.

Re-read your file. When you live with a case for a long time, it is amazing how you can forget how things were. It can be like looking back over your life – you think you remember, but only when you look at old photos do the details come back. You need that fresh recall of the case, not a general hazy recollection.

Get your file in order. Make sure there are no loose pages and all papers are filed in the right place. Flag up significant documents or notes of important events, so you can turn them up quickly if need be. One expert witness went to the High Court carrying all her papers, not in a file but in a heap. Walking up to the witness box, she dropped the whole pile. The court had to rise while she and her instructing solicitor scrabbled about the floor picking up papers and trying to work out what order they should go in. You can imagine the judge's impression of that expert.

Take your file to the court building with you in case you need to check up on something which is not in your statement. Imagine being pressed about a precise detail which is not in your statement and that you cannot remember without checking the file – but the file is in the office, 40 miles away. How happy is the judge with you?

However, do not take your file into the witness box – you are unlikely to need it in any event as your statement is already in the court bundle – because anything you do take into the box can be inspected by the other parties. This could result in a fishing expedition, with everyone trawling through your entire file to see if they can find anything of use to them, causing delay and irritation to all involved. If, however, during your evidence it becomes essential to check a particular point in your file, you can ask the judge for permission to find the relevant document, which you will then need to show to the other parties.

Focus your thinking

Among all the last minute frantic preparations, take some time to reflect on exactly what the case is about. Get the key issues absolutely clear in your mind – what do you want to say to the court? Try summing up the essence of the case to a colleague in a few sentences. Think of three key things which, if nothing else, you want to get across to the court. Keep these in mind when you are in the witness box to keep you on track and help you deal with questions.

Get a clear mental image of the child concerned; remind yourself of what he looks like, his personality and his needs. Think of him before you go to court and keep him in mind throughout the case – after all, he is the reason you are doing this.

Meet your lawyer

Have a meeting with your legal team (known as a 'conference with counsel' if a barrister is instructed). Prepare together for negotiations outside court and for anticipated challenges in court. The lawyer is not allowed to coach you or rehearse your answers with you – you are the witness and it has to be your evidence, not the lawyer's – but there is nothing wrong with anticipating together how the case might proceed. On the other hand, you can coach your lawyer. Help him to ask the right questions of you and the other witnesses, and suggest how he might deal with the parents, who you know far better than he does.

There are always some surprises in court and some questions you could never have anticipated. But some challenges are easily predicted: you only qualified a month ago, how can you be competent to handle this case? The case was unallocated for three months so your authority could not have been very concerned – if it was good enough then why not now?, and so on. Some challenges are apparent from the evidence filed by other parties, for example, if the parents say that no one explained the concerns to them, or no services were provided.

Prepare for the challenges you expect, but don't practise your answers to such an extent that they sound like a rehearsed script. That comes across as false, and spontaneity is important in court. However, if you have not prepared for the challenges you know will come, you will have no spare brain space to deal with the genuine surprise developments.

Preparing yourself

Look the part

Knowing you look right gives you confidence. At the risk of sounding like your mother, it is obviously sensible to decide in advance what you are going to wear and make sure everything is clean and in good order. If you expect to be in court for several days, you need some variation of outfits, all of which need to be clean and presentable. The last thing you need on the morning of court when you are already feeling anxious is to discover that your shoes need cleaning or you have just laddered your last pair of tights (take a spare pair with you, too). Some social workers complain that their salaries do not allow them to buy expensive suits, but designer labels are not required; it is quite possible to be smart on a budget.

It is amazing how, when you are already nervous, an apparently insignificant problem can throw you – one advocate, leaving for court very early one morning, got dressed in the dark to avoid disturbing her family. It was only when she arrived that, to her horror, she noticed that she was wearing one navy and one black shoe. For the rest of the day, she could not get out of her mind the idea that the entire court was focusing on her feet. Check your appearance before you leave home.

Think about the image you want to convey. Like it or not, first impressions are formed on the basis of appearance, and judges and magistrates are only human. The impression you want to convey is of a competent, serious professional and you may also want to counteract the stereotypical image of social workers, all baggy jumpers and sandals. You might feel these points are too obvious even to be made, but at least one Children's Guardian has attended the High Court wearing a denim dress and a bright red cardigan. Another Guardian appeared at court looking so unshaven, rumpled and grubby that at first sight the local authority's barrister mistook him for the abusive father in the case!

Colours should be sober, clothes formal (smart trousers are perfectly acceptable for women) and appearance conventional; court is not the place for self-expression. After all, you are not there in your own right – you are representing your authority and your profession and you are there for the child. You want to be noticed and remembered for the quality of your evidence, not the way you look. A magistrate has recounted how a young female advocate appeared before the Bench in an extremely low cut blouse. Imagine the first five minutes' discussion in the magistrates' retiring room – 'Did you see what she was wearing?' – not a word about the case!

Avoid potentially distracting items like dangly earrings or extravagant jewellery. Some judges and magistrates have 'pet hates' (such as pierced noses or eyebrows, joke socks or cartoon character ties) and antagonising the decision-maker before you have even opened your mouth is not the best start. Having her hair dyed the colours of the rainbow for charity just before appearing in the High Court was not the best plan for one witness.

As well as image, think about comfort. It is a good idea to choose an outfit you know to be comfortable rather than wearing something for the first time. You may spend a considerable time in the witness box so five-inch stilettos may not be the best choice. Many people get hot when they are nervous, so consider wearing a sleeveless blouse or shirt under your jacket. One excellent and experienced witness's top tip for court work is 'wear comfortable pants'!

One advantage of wearing clothes of a type you might not normally choose is that it is like putting on a uniform or costume. It helps you get into role and to adopt your professional persona. It also means that when it is all over you can take it off again and relax.

Before leaving for court, look at yourself in a full-length mirror, stand up straight, look confident and see yourself as an assured, professional witness.

Eat, sleep and relax!

Think of the sort of advice mothers give before their offspring take exams and apply it to yourself. Getting a good night's sleep before court is a sensible start. The scent of lavender is reputed to aid sleep, as is using a hop pillow. Alternatively a long soak in a hot bath, or milky drink before bed might work for you. Sitting up till 3 am 'revising' is never a good plan. Nutritionists all seem to be unanimous that a decent breakfast is essential.

If you are nervous, try using a relaxation tape, practise yoga or t'ai chi or do some exercise. Some swear by Bach Rescue Remedy. However, alcohol and drugs are best avoided. You know what works for you, and what temptations you are likely to succumb to, so be honest with yourself and be sensible.

Dealing with nerves

Nerves are natural, especially when performing a task for the first time – remember your first Case Conference or home visit – your first court appearance is no different. Judges and magistrates understand that witnesses are nervous, and remember that they also had a first day in court.

As for an interview or exam a level of anxiety is natural, even desirable, and a witness who is not nervous to a degree is worryingly complacent and unlikely to perform well. Nerves can be healthy – they heighten your awareness and speed up your reactions. Many people think more clearly and quickly when they are keyed up. Adopt a positive attitude to your nervous feelings. Naturally, you will be a lot less nervous if you are well prepared and know what to expect than if you are entering completely into the unknown.

Remember that no one else can see how you feel inside, and nerves often show far less than you imagine. It is amazing how often, after giving evidence in real life or role play, social workers say they felt terribly nervous, yet they appeared to observers to be quite calm and controlled.

Don't assume either that you are the only person in court who is nervous. Everyone there is performing an important task and should be conscious of that fact. Even the advocates are at least keyed up and some extremely nervous, though you might not know it. One highly experienced barrister when cross-examining twiddles her fingers behind her back, betraying her nerves. However, the judge sees only her utterly composed and confident front. The image to remember is that of the swan, gliding majestically on the surface, but paddling like fury underneath. You, too, need to be that swan.

The judge or magistrates may well be anxious or worried too – imagine being in their shoes, having the responsibility of deciding a child's future. And never forget that the people feeling the worst of all in court are the parents, who stand to lose their child. Get your own nerves into perspective.

Seek support

Rally your troops around you and ask for the support you need, both professional and personal. Make sure your colleagues and your family understand that you have a challenge ahead. Have a reward or a treat ready for when it is all over – it gives you something to look forward to.

Practical preparation

Clear your diary

A working day of 10 am to 4 pm doesn't sound too bad does it? You can surely fit in a meeting before court and a visit or two afterwards plus some quick phone calls at lunchtime, can't you? Don't even try it – you will get distracted and delayed. You need to focus on the case in court and nothing else.

Court work is exhausting, so don't be surprised if you are much more tired than you expect; it is a very concentrated and intense day. Make sure your supervisor knows about your court commitment and makes necessary allowances, including ensuring that your other appointments are covered for you.

Prepare for a late finish

Court cases are usually scheduled to finish at 4 pm, but often more time is needed to allow a witness to finish his evidence or a suitable point to be reached for a break so the court sits on for a while. Courts have been known to continue sitting well into the evening, until 11.30 pm on at least one occasion.

Have contingency plans in place – you are hardly likely to give of your best if you are worrying about who will collect your child from school. One social worker involved in a case which was running over phoned school to explain she was stuck in court and her daughter was to go to her auntie's after school. The next day the mortified teenager was approached by the pastoral care teacher asking if there were problems at home. Make it clear that you are in court as a witness or people assume the worst!

Plan your journey

Even experienced lawyers, amazingly, sometimes turn up at the wrong court – one barrister arrived at Colchester County Court only to find he should have been in Winchester! Nothing is less conducive to a calm professional performance than going to the wrong place, then arriving late, flushed and flustered and having to apologise before you start.

Don't assume all hearings in the same case will be in the same court. The case could be transferred up or the venue could change for any number of practical reasons, and sometimes this happens literally the day before the hearing. Always check exactly where you should be going – get the court's address, phone number and a map. Contact your legal team the day before court to check on any last minute changes or developments. Many towns have more than one court – Magistrates', Crown and County – all in different buildings, often on opposite sides of town. If you just rely on going to the town and asking directions to the court, you are bound to be sent to the wrong one.

Few courts have parking facilities, so you need to know where to park. Have a couple of options available, remembering that things like market days or school holidays can have a considerable impact. Take into account traffic conditions at the time of day when you will be travelling, and listen to local radio for news of any hold-ups. Don't forget loose change for meters. Similar considerations apply to public transport, including checking for cancellations and engineering works, as well as working out how to get from the station/bus stop to court.

Take your mobile phone with you, ensuring it is charged up and has enough credit. Programme in the telephone numbers for the court and your legal adviser so if you are running late you can phone ahead – at least then everyone is forewarned and you will feel less panicked. Remember, too, to know how to contact your senior wherever she will be on the day in case you need advice or a decision has to be made.

Double check the time of your hearing and don't assume that each hearing will be at the same time as the last. Professionalism includes being on time. There is work to be done outside court before the case starts and your advocate cannot do anything without you. Aim to arrive well before the case is due to start – half an hour is an absolute minimum unless your lawyer says otherwise.

People will notice when you arrive. At least one usher keeps a mental note of when social workers arrive for court. When she hears the name of the worker on a case, she (invariably accurately) predicts whether she will arrive on time or keep everyone waiting. If the usher knows, you can be absolutely sure that everyone else in the court does too. What kind of reputation do you want to establish?

Arrange where to meet your team

Some court buildings are enormous. It will not fill you with confidence if you start your day wandering like a lost lamb trying to find your team. Arrange a meeting point in advance, and know exactly who you are going to meet, including what they look like if you have not met before. The High Court in London is a Victorian Gothic rabbit warren and, especially for a first visit, it is best not to try to find your own way to the court room, but arrange to meet at the main entrance.

Find your way around the court building early in the day. Locate the toilets – it is amazing what nerves can do to the digestive system! Notice if there is more than one set of toilets available; sometimes it is worth walking a bit further to avoid an awkward encounter with a parent in the loo. Similar considerations arise for smokers; there is often only one smoking room, so it may be best to smoke outside. If you leave your team before the case is called in, remember to let them know where you are going – the case is bound to be called into court just when you have popped out for a cigarette!

At court

Behaviour outside court

Why does this matter? Think who might be watching. Courts rarely have enough individual conference rooms for all the parties in all the cases in court that day, and you may be in the same large waiting area as the parents and their advocates.

Be aware of the impression you are conveying and put on your professional 'hat' right from the moment you enter the building. Remain conscious of your behaviour until you leave at the end of the day. You are representing your authority, the child, yourself and your profession all day, not just when you are in the witness box, and people who matter start forming impressions of you from the outset.

One social worker is sitting in the corner, reading and re-reading her files with an air of desperation, wringing her hands and biting her nails. How does the opposing advocate feel? She has made his day already! Another social worker arrives late looking a mess, keeps dropping things and has to borrow a pen. Does she look competent and organised? A third breezes in, chats loudly, has a laugh with the Children's Guardian, then shows everyone the latest photographs of her lovely children. How sensitive and professional does she appear?

Always be very mindful of confidentiality, especially if poor facilities mean that you are obliged to discuss matters in a general waiting area. Get out of earshot of others, but if this is impossible at least refrain from mentioning any names or identifying details. Often you will see other professionals at court who are involved in a different case with you – lawyers often find that they can catch up on several cases at once at court, as all the local specialists are there. This can be useful, but never discuss a case in front of anyone not entitled to hear about it.

Seeing the parents at court

Social workers often ask whether they should talk to parents outside court. Clearly it would be inappropriate to have a jolly chat with the parents then go into the witness box and outline their failings in glorious Technicolor. It may also create the wrong impression if you are seen to be talking earnestly to the parents, as if you are putting pressure on them to change their position. On the other hand, it would be frankly rude and unprofessional to ignore them completely, especially when you have been working closely with them for months.

The best course is to prepare in advance – tell the parents that when you are at court you will not be able to spend any time with them as you each have to talk to your lawyers and that the court day is different from your normal work with them. This way they will not be surprised when you greet them courteously then move on. Except in cases where you judge that the parents may react in such a hostile manner that even greeting them would be provocative, you should at least acknowledge their presence.

Safety considerations

Aggression in court is in fact extremely rare – it is remarkable how the formal atmosphere of the court building can improve the behaviour of even the most difficult client. Parents are more often distressed and emotional than aggressive. However, it is always sensible to consider risks and if you have concerns about any possible misbehaviour, voice them as early as possible. Your health and safety are important considerations for your employer, quite apart from the fact that you are unlikely to perform well if you are worried.

Unfortunately, the Court of Appeal showed a frankly scandalous lack of concern for social work witnesses in one case[1], expressing the view that the threat of violence from adults who faced permanent separation from their children was a 'professional hazard of social work and not exceptional'. If the case had concerned a police officer or nurse would the court have described the threat of violence as just an acceptable risk of the job?

Despite this, the courts you appear in day to day are likely to have more concern for your safety. Courts do not, however, have security staff or police routinely available. Arrangements can be made if there is a significant risk but the court must be notified in advance. Alert your legal representatives to your concerns immediately and ask them to put necessary steps in hand.

Always take sensible precautions for your own safety. Never be persuaded to give a parent a lift to court in your own car – even the most docile person may become agitated in such a stressful situation. Getting a client to court is the parent's solicitor's job and he can claim Legal Aid for his client's journey to court; it is not your problem.

Waiting around before court can heighten tension. If there are enough interview rooms available, parents and local authority can wait separately. If not, make sure that as much physical space separates the two sides as possible, and take particular care during breaks.

In court, the usual seating arrangements often mean that social workers and parents sit close to one another. These arrangements can be changed to ensure that there are other people, such as legal representatives, acting as a buffer zone between you. It just needs someone to think of it so don't wait for someone else to raise the issue.

During the hearing, it is the court's job to ensure parties' behaviour is appropriate and not intimidating. Anyone who misbehaves could find himself excluded from court or held to be in contempt of court. In addition, the court will form a clear impression of the person concerned, and take it into account in its decision.

After court, make sure you are not followed to your car. If emotions are running high, either leave court quickly before the parents or wait until they are well clear of the building. Court buildings usually have more than one exit and it has been known on rare occasions for the local authority representatives to be ushered out of a staff exit to avoid confrontation.

Think carefully about your work with the family after court, particularly in the first few sessions after the court's decision.

---

1   *Re W (care proceedings) (witness anonymity)* [2003] 1FLR 329, Court of Appeal, p.334 [13].

Parents' lawyers

Never get into discussion with the lawyers for the other parties except in the presence of your own lawyer. It is, in fact, professionally improper for a lawyer to speak to another lawyer's client, so they should not attempt to approach you in any event. However, some seem to forget that social workers are effectively parties and clients of the local authority's lawyers, so it is possible that someone may approach you quite genuinely – or they may be trying to take advantage. Do not get drawn into discussions about the case and make it clear that you will only talk with your own representative present.

Waiting

One feature of court work is that there is always a lot of waiting around to be done. In the County Court, contested hearings are usually in the 10.30 am list, but the judge also has a 10 am list consisting of supposedly short matters, and complications and emergencies often arise. Your own case may also need more time for discussions or for documents to be drafted before it is ready to go into court.

If you are a witness giving a discrete piece of evidence (not the key worker) you have to wait outside court until it is your turn to go into the witness box. Your advocate will try his best to give you an idea of when you are expected to be heard, but estimating how long evidence will take is more art than science, and the witnesses before you may take more or less time than predicted.

Whenever you are at court, take something to keep yourself occupied while waiting. Re-reading your statement is a good start, but only goes so far – a bit like revising before an exam, there comes a point where no more will go in. Some have tried working on other cases which seems like a productive use of time, but the problem is that after a couple of hours' wait, you only have a moment's notice before you are in action, and your head is filled with the wrong case. Instead, it may be the perfect opportunity to catch up on your backlog of professional journals – that way, your mind stays on professional matters while not being distracted from the case in question.

Finally, the moment arrives when the usher announces your case. In care proceedings to preserve confidentiality the case number, rather than the parties' names, is called.

Walking into court

The parties take their places in court before the judge or magistrates enter, so as key worker you have time to find your place and settle down. You will probably sit beside your advocate in the FPC or behind him in the County or High Court.

Other witnesses have to remain outside court until their turn to give evidence. If you are in this position, the usher calls you by name into court. Everyone else, judge/magistrates included, is already in place when you walk in, so all eyes are on you from the word go. The danger is that you walk into the courtroom looking like a rabbit blinking in the headlights unless you know in advance what the court room looks like and where you have to go.

If you have never been to the particular court before, arrive early and ask the usher (who usually wears a black gown) to show you the court room, explain who sits where and point out which witness box is being used on the day. You can then start your 'performance' as a confident, composed professional from the moment you enter the court room.

Behaviour in court

Remember that the judge or magistrates can see the entire courtroom, not just the witness. They notice and take into account everything they observe – the parent who is angry or laughs inappropriately, the lawyer who has kicked off his shoes and is doodling, the social worker who huffs and puffs at other people's evidence. Your behaviour must be discreet, respectful and professional throughout.

Be an active client. Don't just sit back and let your lawyer get on with it. Discuss the progress of the case during any breaks and make suggestions including ideas of topics or questions to put to witnesses. If necessary, pass messages to him during the hearing, but do so discreetly – don't noisily tear out sheets of paper and wave them in front of him as this will distract and irritate the judge. It is your case, so make sure you play a full role.

Chapter 10

Giving Evidence

Presentation

The content of your evidence is obviously of vital importance. If you have a weak case, the best presentation in the world cannot save it. However, the converse is not true and poor preparation and presentation can undermine even a strong case.

When you take the stand to give your evidence, remember that a substantial percentage of your message is conveyed not through words but through voice and body language. It is not just what you say but how you say it that matters.

Use every trip to court, whether as observer or participant, as a learning experience. Perform a critical observation of every witness you see – are they impressive or not? Why? What would you like to emulate or avoid? You might find the suggested witness observation checklist in Appendix 2 helpful.

Impressive witnesses start as they mean to go on. From the moment they take the stand, they are composed, professional and assured.

Addressing your evidence

If you remember nothing else from this book, remember this. The single top tip to being an effective witness is to address everything you say to the decision-maker(s). In family cases, this means the judge or magistrates; in the Crown Court, this means the jury.

Why?

- Think who needs to know the answer? Everyone else in the courtroom already knows what they think the outcome should be – and it matters not a jot. Only the judge's opinion matters, so give him the information he needs to make the right decision.

- How do the judge or magistrates feel if no one looks at them? Imagine being a magistrate, sitting in court while an advocate and witness have an apparently private exchange, looking at each other and never addressing you. How long would you remain engaged and concentrating on the case? Magistrates and judges are only human after all, and after a while are likely to feel excluded and struggle to maintain concentration.

- Cross-examination is all about control. The opposing advocate is trying to control you, and perhaps the most powerful tool he has is eye contact. If the witness is looking at him the advocate can interrupt just by using body language. Try it yourself – you can stop someone in full flow just by taking in a breath, raising your eyebrows and signalling that it is your turn to speak. Most people are so polite that they obediently stop and allow you to take over. Advocates can also try to undermine the witness by feigning boredom, exasperation or incredulity at their answers – this does not work if the witness is not looking in their direction. Break the eye contact and you break the control.

- Who would you rather talk to – a hostile advocate or an at least neutral and possibly interested and encouraging judge or magistrate?

- You may get some feedback from the judge or magistrates – nods, frowns, puzzled looks – which may indicate how your evidence is being received and whether you are getting your message across and you may even get an indication of approval or understanding. A foster carer was once cross-examined in an unnecessarily aggressive manner, and the magistrates physically leaned towards her – they would have given her a hug if they could! There was no doubt where the court's sympathy lay, and that the advocate was actually undermining his case by his aggression, but the witness would not have known that if she had only been looking at the advocate. Don't worry, however, if you get no feedback at all; it is a matter of personal style – some courts make a point of remaining studiously neutral, and at least one judge made everyone in court wonder if he was still alive, let alone listening (although of course he was).

- It shows courtesy to the court and gives everyone present the message that you are a professional witness who understands court etiquette.

Watch other people giving evidence, and you will see how effective this technique is and how witnesses who do not use it put themselves at a disadvantage. See if witnesses manage to maintain the technique throughout their evidence – sometimes people start well, but lose focus as they are challenged or if they become anxious, riled or defensive; then the advocate has the upper hand. As things become more challenging it becomes even more important to keep control.

Of course, it feels unnatural to be asked a question by one person and address the answer to someone else. We are trained from childhood to look at the person who is speaking to us, and witnesses sometimes worry that they seem rude if they do not look at the advocate. This is not the case, but it is far better to risk rudeness to an advocate than to ignore the judge or magistrates. This technique does not come naturally, especially if you are feeling stressed or under pressure. So how is it done?

The key technique is to angle your body towards the judge/magistrates. Do this from the moment you enter the witness box, and make sure that every single word you utter, starting from the oath or affirmation, is addressed to them and no one else. Point your feet and hips towards the judge/magistrates and you will naturally look in that direction. When an advocate asks you a question, turn your head and shoulders towards him to receive the question, but as it is uncomfortable to stand in that twisted position for long, you naturally turn back towards the judge/magistrates to give your answer. In the Family Proceedings Court, witnesses remain seated to give evidence so angle your chair, if you can, to face the Bench. If the seat is fixed, place your bottom so your body is angled towards the Bench.

As it is such an artificial exercise, it is not easy to use this technique without practice. Try it out with the co-operation of two colleagues. Place yourself so that you cannot look at both colleagues at the same time. One person asks you questions, and you address the answers to the other, who listens passively. Start with unchallenging questions, such as your name, professional address and qualifications, just to get into the habit of looking from one to the other. Once you feel more comfortable about the principle, ask your questioner to step up a gear and start to tackle more challenging subjects, and to be provocative, perhaps raising religion, politics or something likely to stir you up. Keep calm and continue to address your answers to the 'magistrate'.

Taking the oath/affirmation

The first thing you have to do as a witness is to take the oath (religious) or affirmation (non-religious). It does not matter which you choose, but know in advance which you want to do. Ushers often assume that witnesses will swear on the New Testament unless they say otherwise. Holy Books and appropriate forms of words for other religions are available, but tell the usher in advance if this applies to you – otherwise you could be standing in the box in court 1 waiting for the usher to run to court 37 to get the relevant documents – hardly designed to calm your nerves.

At this point, the script is there for you and it is difficult to say the wrong thing, although it has been done – one social worker promised to tell a judge 'the truth, the whole truth and anything but the truth'! Use this chance to get yourself composed and get your voice working. Make sure you address the judge or magistrates from the word go, making eye contact although without fixing them with an unnerving unblinking stare. Start as you mean to go on.

Should you sit or stand?

Witnesses always stand while taking the oath or affirmation, whichever court they are in. In the Family Proceedings Court, witnesses are then invited to sit, as the whole case is conducted with all participants seated, advocates included. In the County and High Courts the presumption is that witnesses remain standing to give evidence, but the judge may ask if you would prefer to sit. It is up to you, but bear the following points in mind:

- The advocates stand when asking you questions. It does not take much amateur psychology to work out who has the power if one person is sitting and the other standing. Do you want to put yourself at a disadvantage from the start?

- Witness boxes are generally designed for a witness who is standing, not sitting. Unless they are particularly tall, witnesses practically disappear if they sit down in some courts. Try appearing authoritative when you are peering over the edge of the box!

- Anyone who sings will tell you that vocal production is generally better if you are standing upright so you can breathe freely and your diaphragm is not scrunched up as it may be when you are sitting down, especially if you hunch over.

- Standing up straight gives an air of confidence and helps remind you that you are performing an important task.

Examination in chief

After the oath, the next stage is examination in chief, when you are asked questions by your own advocate. Your first task is to confirm your own name and professional address, so there is a good chance that you know the answer, however nervous you are!

Your advocate then asks you to confirm your statement(s). Do not take your own copy into the witness box but use the court bundle, which is indexed and paginated and contains copies of all the papers in the case.

Sometimes there are problems with bundles such as incorrect pagination, missing pages or faulty photocopying. These are simple clerical errors, which easily occur – imagine photocopying and paginating thousands of pages – but they cause judicial irritation. None of this is your problem. Rise serenely above it. If you are asked to turn to a page in the bundle only to find that it looks wrong, don't soldier on, just point out the problem and let someone else sort it out.

Take your time to focus on the statement, make sure it is the right one, and remember that this is your opportunity to correct any mistakes in the statement.

Evidence in chief is brief, probably consisting of only a few questions to update the evidence since your last statement and to comment on the Guardian's report. Use it to the full as an opportunity to ensure that you are facing the right direction and expressing yourself clearly.

Voice

We tend to take our voices for granted, and assume that speaking is something we learned to do when we were toddlers. In fact very few of us know how to breathe properly or ever give any thought as to how we actually produce the sound we make. We rarely hear ourselves as others hear us. Try recording yourself talking on tape and play it back to hear how your voice sounds. How clearly do you speak? How quickly do you speak? Do you have any habits or vocal tics, 'you know', 'like', 'erm'? Don't be the last person to know you have an irritating habit which you could easily overcome.

Our voices are vital tools of our trade which are too often neglected, so as part of your professional development programme consider going on a public speaking or presentation workshop or try singing or drama classes. How you speak in court is crucial for the most basic and obvious reason – the best evidence in the world is wasted if no one can hear it. Your voice is also an important part of the overall impression you convey. Imagine a witness who speaks in a timid, apologetic little voice which the court has to strain to hear. Does she inspire you with confidence in her professional expertise and competence? Picture a witness who gabbles and races through his evidence – does he impress you as composed, organised and thoughtful?

Be aware of your surroundings and adjust your voice accordingly as court rooms vary enormously in size. Some are no bigger than an average meeting room whereas others, especially in the higher courts, are large rooms with high ceilings. Do not rely on the microphones you see in the County and High Courts as they only record the evidence and do not amplify your voice.

You know whether you naturally have a quiet or strong voice. Bear in mind that sometimes an effect of nerves is that people speak more quietly than normal. If you cannot be heard in court, the judge or one of the advocates will ask you to speak up. This will not boost your confidence. If you have to be asked more than once it becomes irritating for all involved, judge included, and there comes a point where everyone gives up trying to persuade you to speak audibly and your evidence is effectively lost.

If you naturally speak quietly, it will feel strange to you to project your voice. You need to aim to speak at such a level that to you it feels too loud and to everyone else that will probably be about right. Practice as often as you can before going to court – with everything else to think about on the day, it is not the best moment to try speaking up for the first time. Start immediately, and try speaking out loudly in the privacy of your own home or car. Use the opportunity of any meetings you attend to make a conscious effort to project your voice more than usual. Find a large room and ask a helpful colleague to see how well you can be heard from a distance – not just once – such things take practice. Try reading the words of the oath or affirmation, giving your name, professional address and qualifications, then move on to a summary of your concerns about a particular child. The more you can get used to speaking out confidently the better.

Get your voice working on the way to court. Sing in the shower, talk back to the radio in the car and practise any vocal exercises you know. As soon as you get in the witness box, start as you mean to go on and take the oath in a strong confident voice. Don't mumble – open your mouth and enunciate clearly. Remember that you will be giving evidence for some time and you need to sustain your volume throughout. Sometimes witnesses start confidently enough then lose momentum and volume as they go along. It can be a real indicator that a witness is tiring or losing confidence if her voice starts to drop, and that only encourages a cross-examining advocate, so throughout your evidence periodically remind yourself to keep speaking up. If you feel your confidence starting to sap, that is the time to redouble your efforts to at least sound confident.

Diction

This is not an elocution exam. You do not have to speak Queen's English or have impeccable diction, but you do have to be understood. Accents often become stronger through nerves, and this is exacerbated if you also speak quickly or mumble. If you are aware that you have a marked accent, don't feel you have to put on a voice which is not your own, but be very careful to enunciate as clearly as you can and to speak at a measured pace. Again, a frank colleague can help you practise.

Pace

Another common nervous reaction is to speak too quickly. Witnesses sometimes gabble in the anxiety to get out everything they want to say, but end up defeating the object as their evidence gets lost in the rush. In the Family Proceedings Court, the only record of the proceedings is the handwritten note kept by the clerk. Even in the County and High Courts where proceedings are tape recorded, everyone (judge included) keeps their own notes of evidence. While you should not go at dictating speed people still need to be able to keep up with you. Clerks have been heard to cry out 'watch the pen!' meaning do not start on the next sentence until he has caught up.

If you know you speak quickly at the best of times make a particular effort to slow down and to pause more often. It may have to feel unnaturally slow to you to get to the point where it sounds right to others. Try recording yourself and taking notes when you play it back – can you keep up?

Start by reading the oath at a measured pace and be sure to keep it up. As with volume, witnesses often start well then forget as time goes on, especially if they become in any way animated. Witnesses losing their cool – whether riled, defensive or emotional – tend to speed up, so this is a real signal to cross-examining advocates that the witness is losing composure and it is time to turn up the heat.

Silence is also part of communication. Don't be afraid to pause. Take your time to think; avoid rushing. Take a deep breath as this not only helps you to speak more strongly but also calms your nerves. Try to breathe from your diaphragm rather than taking shallow, panting breaths. If your mouth gets dry, take a sip of water (there should be a glass on the witness stand – if there isn't, ask for one). You can also make your mouth water by running your tongue over the front of your teeth, gently biting the tip of your tongue or just by imagining yourself sucking on a lemon.

Tone

As for written work, the message is conveyed not just by what you say, but how you say it. Listeners pick up a lot of subtle information about you and how you are feeling from your voice. Keep calm and controlled – avoid being pompous, defensive, angry or emotional. Remember, too, to keep the audience interested by varying your pitch and tone – no one wants to listen to a monotonous robot for long. It helps if you remember that you are talking to real people who just happen to be magistrates, telling them what you know, rather than giving a speech to a vast impersonal audience. Always keep your child client in the forefront of mind.

Language

The language you use in the witness box is important, first to ensure that your evidence is readily understood by everyone in court and second to convey an air of professionalism and competence.

Avoid jargon. Specialist terms may not be understood by everyone in court or, worse still, people listening may think they know what a term means but may have misunderstood completely. A magistrate who does not understand a term is unlikely to want to look foolish by asking what it means. Stick to plain, ordinary English to get your message across.

However, do retain a level of formality in your speech. You are giving evidence on oath, not chatting to your friends; this is a formal, important occasion. Avoid vulgarity. You might think this so obvious that it does not need to be said, but apparently not. One psychiatrist giving evidence in care proceedings said, 'If you treat children like shit, they turn into shit.' What would be your reaction on hearing that from an expert witness? Probably the same as the judge, who exclaimed, 'That is language I might expect to hear from a juvenile delinquent, not a consultant psychiatrist!' and demanded a letter of apology. You can imagine how much reliance the judge placed on that witness's evidence.

It can sometimes be necessary to use a swear word if repeating the precise words someone used. It can be significant evidence, for example, that the child's speech is very limited save for a fluent knowledge of vulgarities. It is no good being coy, saying that someone 'was rude' or 'used foul language' – that is far too subjective. Instead, signal to the court that you know that this is not the language you would normally use in court – you could say, 'If I may, I will use her exact words. She said...'.

Posture and body language

Stand or sit up straight. If you are standing, adopt an open stance with your feet slightly apart, in line with your hips – this should feel comfortable and make you feel grounded. Keep your shoulders back and avoid hunching over. Keep you chin up (literally and metaphorically) and look people confidently in the eye. Before you go to court, visualise yourself looking assured and composed and retain that mental image. If you are sitting, sit up straight, neither hunched over nor slouching – take care not to become too relaxed.

Be careful what messages you convey with your hands – they can aid communication or add expression with an occasional gesture to reinforce a point but they can also give away nerves or agitation if you tap your fingers, wring your hands or grip desperately to the edge of the witness box. You would look disrespectfully casual if your hands were in your pockets or defensive if you stood with your arms folded. Your hands can distract attention if they wave around as if you are doing semaphore, or if you constantly repeat a particular gesture like a visual tic. Some witnesses gesture more when they get carried away or lose their composure – another give-away sign for the predatory advocate. Some of us have a habit of fiddling with our pens. It is very difficult to retain professional composure while desperately trying to rub ink off your hands and to address the court with an air of authority despite having bright blue fingers (a painful personal experience). If you are an inveterate pen fiddler, take a pencil – at least they don't leak.

Don't think that you have to stand in the witness box immobile like a soldier standing to attention, but do be aware of what your posture and gestures communicate. Some people find it comforting to rest their fingertips lightly together (not clamped together as if you are praying for help); it is suggested that this makes the 'chi' energy flow smoothly through the body.

Become aware of your own habits – stand in front of a full length mirror and describe to yourself in the mirror your concerns for a particular child. Watch yourself while you are speaking and note your own body language. Ask a helpful colleague to watch you and be honest about how you come across or, better still, if you can bear it, video yourself.

Answering questions

Think again about how you want to appear as a witness. Words like calm, professional, reasonable, clear and thoughtful probably spring to mind.

Listen to the question

Focus carefully on the question you are actually asked. Sometimes witnesses seem to hear the start of the question then jump to their own conclusion of what the advocate is asking. Concentrate on the exact words the advocate uses and listen out for subtle differences – for example, you might be happy to agree that a parent listens to your advice, but not that she takes your advice.

Ask for clarification or repetition where necessary

If you do not hear the question, ask for it to be repeated. If you do not understand the question, don't guess at what you think it meant – you might have the wrong end of the stick. It is not your problem if the advocate cannot express himself clearly, and it is not your job to help him out. Ask for the question to be repeated or rephrased. You will probably find that no one else in court understood it either! Advocates hate being asked to repeat a question, especially when they know that it wasn't the most elegant question ever posed.

Take your time

You are not on Mastermind – it is not an exercise to answer as many questions as possible in a limited time. You will not get it over with more quickly by rushing; on the contrary, ill-considered answers could lead to you spending longer in the witness box.

Consider each question and your response to it. You do not have to answer instantly, and should not be afraid of a moment or two of silence in the court room. If you feel uncomfortable pausing when all eyes are on you, try taking a sip of water (just a sip, not huge gulps or you will need a comfort break), or looking for a moment at your statement in front of you. You could try using a phrase along the lines of 'let me take a moment to consider', so that the room is not in silence, but you are still giving yourself time to think.

If you don't know – say so

Never make things up. Don't speculate or hypothesise. If you do not know the answer, say so. Don't ask, as one witness did, 'Can you give me a clue?' If you cannot remember, say so, but do feel free to use your statement to refresh your memory – court is not a memory test.

Answer the question

Do answer the question actually asked. Don't try to avoid it, give a stock answer no matter what the question may be, or answer the question you wish you had been asked. Think of politicians you have seen doing this in interviews and remember how irritating it is. No one is fooled.

Don't try to second-guess where the advocate is going. He has a game plan and has thought questions out several moves ahead, like a game of chess, but you don't have to. Trying too hard to spot the direction of the advocate's questions and his ultimate objective can result in a witness looking suspicious or defensive. Take each question as it comes and consider your answer carefully before giving it.

Your job is to answer questions, not to ask them – don't answer a question with a question and never get into an argument.

Know your boundaries

Know the limits of your expertise and of your role in the case. Do not answer a question which is not properly one for you – resist the temptation to try to help out. If a question should be properly addressed to another witness, say so. For example, as a social worker, do not attempt to answer a medical question but suggest that the advocate should ask the paediatrician. If your only role was to observe contact, don't get drawn in to making comments about the child's care plan.

Focus on the child

Always remember what – and who – the case is about. The issue is how the child has been treated and the child's welfare. It is not a trial of your competence as a worker or the efficiency or otherwise of your authority's services. It is not a trial of the behaviour or personalities of the parents – these are only relevant in so far as they affect the child. It is not an issue of whether the parents are morally guilty – they may be utterly blameless, but still unable to care for their child. Try not to get distracted onto other topics – this might be the advocate's very objective – and always try to bring your thoughts and evidence back to what is relevant for the child.

Don't be monosyllabic

Occasional one-word answers can be refreshing, but if your evidence simply consists of single-word responses you fail in your main task of informing the court and could give the impression that you have something to hide or simply do not trust yourself to answer more fully.

Don't ramble

Answers which are too long can lose the court's attention and often stray away from the point and lose coherence. Witnesses who waffle seem unfocused and disorganised, giving the impression that they are not clear thinking in their work either. Keep your answers to the point.

Above all, keep your cool

Stay calm and professional throughout. Keep in control of your emotions. Never show yourself to be angry, upset or irritated, even if that is how you feel inside. Take a deep breath, count to ten, take a sip of water, and always remember to look at the judge or magistrates. Remember you are not on trial; you are there to do a job for the child.

QUESTIONS FOR REFLECTION

* What are your strong points as a witness?
* What do you need to work on?

Chapter 11

Cross-examination

What is cross-examination for?

Contrary to popular belief, cross-examination is not designed just to satisfy lawyers' sadistic tendencies.

Courts are charged with making very difficult and significant decisions. Evidence needs to be tested to ensure that it is reliable. Where more than one version of events is put forward, the court's need to ensure that each is rigorously probed is even more acute.

Asking questions is a natural way to check whether what is being said is true or not – you have certainly done this yourself. Imagine you are faced with a broken window, a football and two children each denying responsibility – what do you do? No doubt you ask each child questions, including a few trick questions, and from their responses (what they say and how they say it) you judge what really happened. The idea that the answers to questions illuminate the path to the truth lies at the heart of our trial system.

In court, however, the questions are asked not by the neutral arbitrator, but by someone who is partisan. His aim is not to get to the objective truth but to his client's subjective version of it, while at the same time undermining the accounts put forward by the other parties.

In the English system parties have the right not just to put their own case but also to challenge the other side's case. This is achieved by cross-examination, which is a vital part of the right to a fair trial. Imagine for a moment being the parent in care proceedings, risking the loss of your child. Wouldn't you want your advocate to ask every possible question and use any available tactic? Do not, therefore, be surprised if that is what parents' advocates do. It is a legitimate part of the process, and it is right as a matter of principle that your case should be strenuously tested. Remind yourself of this if you ever feel upset or angered by a question – wouldn't you do the same thing if the positions were reversed? The advocate is just doing his job, and you must do yours.

In care proceedings where there are multiple parties, every witness is cross-examined by a number of advocates each approaching the case from a different angle. Imagine you are seeking a care order with a care plan of adoption. You are cross-examined by advocates on behalf of:

- the mother, who argues that your concerns are exaggerated and the child should return to her

- the father, who acknowledges some concerns but blames mother and says the child should live with him instead

- the grandmother, who agrees neither parent can cope, but argues the child should come to her instead of being adopted

- the child on the instructions of the Guardian, who accepts your concerns and supports a care order but argues for fostering with contact, not adoption.

The different objectives and standpoints of each party determine the questions the advocates ask you.

Cross-examination questions

As they are designed to achieve a particular outcome, cross-examination questions are different from questions in normal life. Generally we ask a question because we do not know the answer and want to find out, but when a lawyer asks a question in cross-examination, he already knows what the answer will be, or at least what he wants it to be. No advocate should venture into the unknown (known as 'going on a fishing expedition') because he could get an answer which damages his case.

An advocate wants to control the witness – he knows what he wants her to say and his objective is to make her say it. It is no surprise, therefore, to find that cross-examination is full of closed and leading questions. The advocate avoids open questions which put the witness in control and give her the chance to repeat her evidence in chief, emphasising yet again all of his client's faults and failings.

Advocates also know that information is not just conveyed by the words spoken, but also by the witness's demeanour. Questions may be designed, therefore, not just to make the witness say a certain thing, but to behave in a certain way and show herself to be judgemental or arrogant.

You are not a marionette. The advocate wants to control you, but you do not have to let him. His role is to try to shape the evidence his way; your role is to give information – the truth, the whole truth and nothing but the truth – to the court. You do have to answer the advocate's questions, but you do not have to dance to his tune – make sure the evidence you give is your own and as you want it to be.

How advocates prepare

Imagine yourself as advocate for the parent in a case you know well. What is your objective? How do you approach the task?

For a start, an advocate must have a detailed knowledge of the case. He reads and re-reads every page of the bundle and knows exactly what each witness has written in evidence, and how it all fits together – especially where there are gaps, weaknesses and contradictions. If you are the key worker, you have the same bundle as he does, so you should be just as well informed and well prepared. Remember, though, that you have an advantage over even the best advocate – you were there, you saw things with your own eyes, you know this child and this family – he only knows the papers. You should know your own case more intimately than any advocate ever can.

Based on his client's instructions, the advocate develops his own case theory – the version he wants the court to accept – and designs both broad strategy and detailed tactics to get him there. He seeks to undermine the case overall and to challenge the witnesses' credibility and the details of their evidence. He also makes the most of any evidence favourable to his client, no matter who it comes from. He knows what he wants to achieve with each witness individually and how that fits into the whole picture he is trying to create for the court; sometimes he may seek to play one witness off against another. He plans his cross-examination of each witness, aiming to start and finish on a high note every time.

Emphasising strengths

You can always expect this. If there have been 20 difficult, distressing contact sessions and just one which was acceptable, it is no surprise that the parents' advocate emphasises every single detail of the acceptable one. This should already be fully acknowledged in your statement so you can simply refer to the concessions you have already made. Don't be grudging about positives – sometimes social workers seem to fear that anything complimentary said about a parent will undermine their case, whereas in fact the reverse is true – the court appreciates a fair social worker who generously acknowledges a parent's strengths. On the other hand, you must not allow the advocate to take these positives out of all proportion; you need to keep a sense of balance.

If, however, your statement does not mention positives which should fairly be there, you will be portrayed as selective and unfair. In a case involving a young and vulnerable mother, the worker filed a statement full of criticisms and negatives with no concessions. In cross-examination, the worker was asked to outline some of the mother's strengths, which she did, fairly and generously. She was then asked where those points were in her statement. An uncomfortable look crossed her face as she realised that her statement said nothing positive about the mother. She had to concede that this information was not there and it should have been. The questions then followed: if you have left out such important information, what else have you conveniently forgotten? Is your evidence the whole truth or just the bits of the truth you want the court to hear? If you are so critical and negative towards this vulnerable young mum is it any surprise that she found it difficult to work with you?

Undermining social services' case

Contradicting factual evidence

The factual evidence is the foundation of the case. Opinions and recommendations are based on the facts. Therefore, if the court can be persuaded that the factual matrix Social Services rely upon is inaccurate, their conclusions naturally fall. Imagine, for example, a case where a baby has suffered a subdural haemotoma. Social Services base the case on medical opinion that this is a non-accidental shaking injury. If the parents persuade the court that in fact what happened was they accidentally dropped the child down the stairs, the whole case folds. The advocate's objective is to persuade the court to accept his clients' version of the facts.

Sometimes advocates challenge the truth of Social Services' evidence by putting forward a different version of events ('you say the child is indifferent to mother at contact, but in fact she runs to her with open arms'). They rarely suggest that professional witnesses are actually lying – that would alienate the court and generally is implausible –why would a professional lie? More often, they suggest that you 'might be mistaken', or that 'on reflection, perhaps things might have been different', or you might have 'misunderstood or misinterpreted' things. They might offer you an alternative scenario and invite you to accept it, sometimes expressed as 'I put it to you that…'.

Does the advocate really expect you to change your mind? Does he seriously think you will say 'Well, now I think about it, you're right' or 'You guessed it, I made it all up'? He would probably fall over if you did, so why does he ask the question? In fact, he is professionally obliged to put his client's case to you. Where the court is faced with two or more competing versions of events, the witnesses must each be given the chance to comment on the other's account. He cannot later call his client to say that it was you who slapped the child not her, without first giving you the opportunity to consider and confirm or deny that evidence.

Do not be concerned, therefore, about 'I put it to you…' questions. Do not get offended that you are being called a liar. All you need to do is to consider the question and calmly reply that you do not agree with the advocate's proposition and confirm that things were as described in your statement.

However, do not adopt a reflex response of always disagreeing with the advocate. Take time to consider the question as there may be very exceptional circumstances where you might want to accept his suggestion. One health visitor's report included a list of the child's height and weight measurements. There was evidently a mistake in one entry as the figures indicated the child had lost height one month, a unique medical phenomenon. Somehow this had slipped everyone's notice until cross-examination. The advocate invited the witness to accept that this figure must be a typing error, but she insisted it accorded with her records; so it was suggested that her reading on that date had been inaccurate or her equipment was faulty. Instead of gracefully accepting that there must be some mistake, she refused to concede any errors whatsoever and kept on insisting that her evidence was accurate, in spite of the obvious offence to common sense. By so doing, she undermined her own credibility.

Sometimes, the advocate might challenge a witness's recall by asking in considerable detail about a particular incident, seeking to establish that she cannot recollect all or part of the event, and thereby suggesting that her recall is suspect overall. Even if your recall is accurate, the advocate may try to show that it is selective – that you have only remembered or noted those elements which suit your case, showing you to be both judgemental and an unreliable historian.

If you rely on notes, particularly if the event was some time ago, the accuracy of those notes could be challenged, especially if they were not contemporaneous (that is, made at the time) but are a neatened up and edited version prepared for the file. The advantage you have over the parents, however, is that you do at least have notes which were, one hopes, made close to the event. If your recall can be challenged when you do have a record imagine how much more forcefully the same challenge applies to the parents. Parents' solicitors often advise them to keep their own records and diaries of events during the course of proceedings, just as professionals do, but sadly they rarely manage to put that advice into practice.

Contradicting the interpretation of the facts – challenging opinions

If the facts themselves cannot successfully be challenged, the next possibility is to tackle how those facts are applied.

The advocate might challenge the witness's expertise and entitlement to express opinions at all. He will do this, if at all, at the outset of the witness's evidence and the court will hear details of the witness's qualifications and experience to determine whether she is an expert. If not, her opinions will be excluded. Another tactic is to try to undermine the witness's level of expertise – accepting that she has some, but not such as to entitle her to give an authoritative view. This is an obvious approach where, for example, a newly qualified social worker has a different opinion from an experienced Guardian. By emphasising the social worker's lack of experience, the advocate could undermine her confidence as well as suggesting to the court that her recommendations should be treated with caution.

An expert in one field is not entitled to express opinions in another. An advocate may try to entice you to do so, relying on your natural inclination to be helpful – do not be tempted, know your own limits. If a social worker expresses the view that the mother was suffering from paranoid delusions (without a psychiatric diagnosis in place), the next question will be as to when the worker qualified as a psychiatrist as she omitted to mention this in her statement. If a witness does not know her boundaries, her credibility is undermined.

Even if the witness's expertise is accepted, her opinion can be challenged by suggesting that the facts do not lead logically to the conclusion drawn, that certain factors have been given too much or too little weight, or that an alternative conclusion is equally, or more, valid.

Research or theories quoted can be challenged by arguing that the material chosen is inappropriate for the case, and putting forward alternatives; by arguing that the right theory has been wrongly applied; or simply by testing the social worker's depth of knowledge of the tools she has used – if a shaky foundation is exposed, the whole basis of the reasoning starts to crumble.

Scenario 11.1: How an advocate approaches a case

Baby Jack's case turns on physical and emotional neglect. The evidence includes information on unhygienic home conditions and on his mother Kate's failure to provide him with adequate physical or emotional care or appropriate stimulation. Unsuccessful efforts to improve Kate's parenting skills are detailed.

Kate denies many of the allegations but accepts that, due to post-natal depression, she has sometimes been less responsive than she should have been. She has not found Social Services helpful – on the contrary she feels criticised, undermined and disempowered. Now she is receiving treatment for depression and feels able to cope.

What does Kate's advocate want to achieve and how might he do it?

Overall objective: Resist the making of a care order – aim to end proceedings with no order being made.

Case plan:
Step 1 – positives:

1.   Emphasise Kate's strengths.

2.   Show Kate is reasonable and accepts there were some problems.

3.   Her post-natal depression (the cause of the problems) is now being treated.

Step 2 – undermine Social Services' case:

4.   Establish problems were exaggerated.

5.   Show Social Services' approach was unhelpful.

Strategy

1.   With each witness get credit for Kate's positive qualities and good aspects of parenting (if witnesses are balanced and fair, these points should be conceded; if not, this helps towards points 4 and 5). Supplement this with Kate's own sympathetic demeanour in the witness box.

2.   Get acknowledgement that Kate recognises problems, showing insight.

3.   Kate sought treatment for depression; stress medical explanation for difficulties.

4.   Put each incident/criticism Kate denies to Social Services witnesses with alternative version of events and invite concessions; isolate and minimise each individual concern; suggest Social Services is exaggerating concerns, imposing unrealistic standards and being judgemental.

5.   Dissect and criticise Social Services' approach – find fault with services offered and failure to provide different services (e.g. failure to spot depression); attack manner of delivery (critical and judgemental not supportive and constructive). Use social worker's demeanour in the witness box to reinforce this.

Style of questioning

Advocates adopt a variety of styles. To some extent this is a reflection of their personalities and approach. However, better advocates have at their disposal a range of styles and techniques and choose the most effective for the particular witness or the particular moment. It can be disconcerting for a witness who thinks she has got used to the advocate's gentle questioning style suddenly to be faced with a waspish strike, or for a witness who has been warned that a particular advocate is usually aggressive to find a smiling, coaxing questioner.

Aggressive and bullying questioning

Most inexperienced witnesses expect cross-examination to be aggressive; they imagine they will be torn to shreds and left weeping. In fact this is extremely rare. Aggressive or histrionic advocacy is generally counter-productive in the family courts – there is no jury to impress, and the experienced lay bench or professional judge making the decisions favour a less adversarial approach. If they feel a witness is being unfairly intimidated or bullied, they will step in to stop it, and their sympathies then lie more with the witness than the advocate. On the whole, therefore, family advocates tend not to be aggressive or bombastic, instead trying to be (or at least to appear) reasonable and likeable.

Sometimes, however, an advocate might choose to be aggressive, challenging or provocative. This might be because:

- He wants to provoke a particular response from the witness. Imagine the local authority's barrister cross-examining an allegedly aggressive and abusive father. The statements include pages of description of the man's intemperate and unpleasant behaviour, but what could be more powerful than letting the magistrates see him in action for themselves? The barrister might deliberately aim to wind him up and let him go. This should not apply directly to a professional witness, and no amount of provocation should induce an angry or aggressive response from a social worker. However, it might be part of a parent's case that the social worker is hostile to the client, defensive and unwilling to listen, or judgemental and biased. These attitudes might be shown up by aggressive questioning – not just through what the witness says, but the manner in which she says it.

- His client has specifically instructed him to be challenging. He might have advised his client that there is no realistic chance of success, but the client wants to fight nonetheless and wants Social Services to have a hard time in the process. The advocate is doing little more than going through the motions, making a show for his client to give him his day in court.

- The advocate is inexperienced and nervous or is used to appearing in the Crown Court where grandstanding is more acceptable, and he is simply not attuned to the atmosphere of the family court.

- He really has no good points to make and tries to make his case look impressive by lots of sound and fury, signifying nothing.

How to deal with an aggressive advocate

- Never forget that addressing your answers to the judge or magistrates breaks eye contact with the advocate and thus his control. You will feel calmer talking to the judge or magistrates rather than the unpleasant advocate.

- Whatever you do, never ever rise to the bait – that is exactly what he wants you to do, so do not give him the satisfaction. Do not get involved in an argument, answer a question with a question or get defensive. Stay calm at all times and retain your composure.

- Take your time. Aggression often requires a fast pace to be sustained, so break the rhythm. Pause, consider the question, take a deep breath, look at the papers or take a sip of water.

- Feel sorry for the advocate – if this is his best tactic, he must have a very weak case. He is only trying to do his job. Remember that the court is likely to be unimpressed by him and their sympathies will be with you. Don't risk antagonising the court yourself by your demeanour.

- Always remember that the case is not about you – it is about the child. Keep your mind on your objective.

Gentle and smiling questioning

This can be one of the most effective approaches, well suited to the family court. A witness who expects a tough challenge can be lulled into a false sense of security by an apparently unchallenging and sympathetic advocate. This is a particular danger in the Family Proceedings Court where everyone is seated. One experienced social worker was taken completely off her guard by a kind, friendly advocate. The layout of the particular courtroom was such that advocate and witness were sitting opposite each other. The witness forgot to address the Bench, and looked at the friendly, open face of the advocate. It was like an informal chat and the witness was clearly dangerously relaxed; she had forgotten that she was giving evidence on oath to the court. She was then completely wrong-footed when the trap into which she had been so smilingly led was sprung.

Likewise, a mother who allegedly had no control over her very young but dangerously wayward children proved the local authority's case for them thanks to gentle questioning. Criticising or challenging her would have provoked a defensive response, so the advocate sympathised with how difficult it must be to look after these children. The mother told him about all her troubles, including recounting events unknown up to that point even to Social

Services, encouraged all along by the advocate's gentle prompting. She had no idea of the damage she had done to her own case.

How to deal with gentle, friendly cross-examination

Do not be fooled or lulled into thinking that this is anything other than a rigorous test of your evidence. Remain on your guard – without overdoing it and becoming defensive or looking suspicious. Give each question the same degree of consideration and respect as you would if it were asked in a more overtly challenging manner.

It can be very tempting to try to help out someone who seems to be pleasant and friendly – resist the temptation. Don't be drawn into answering questions beyond your expertise or knowledge, into speculation or hypothesis ('if my client manages to stay off drugs') or into comparing one client against another ('many of your other clients must be much more difficult than my client').

It is always nice to be able to agree with someone, and the friendly advocate often puts propositions to the witness which she can agree to – he takes her by the hand and leads her down the garden path. Before you take each step, make sure that you really do want to go in that direction. Often, the first few steps are small and simple and it is no problem to go along with the advocate – but don't get into the habit of agreeing, and watch out for the subtle detour in the path or the giant step too far at the end. Never agree to statements which you would not make of your own accord. Even if you do agree, avoid getting into the habit of replying 'yes' to each question as this leads to the temptation to say 'yes' when the answer should be 'no'. Try using different words for each answer – 'correct', 'that's right', 'quite so', 'I agree'.

Never let yourself be flattered. If an advocate who is not your own starts emphasising how skilful you are or how brilliantly you have worked, remember that he is doing this for a reason, which may not be clear even at the end of your evidence because he may be building up ammunition to fire later at someone else. For example, sometimes parents have a better relationship with one professional, perhaps a family care worker, than another, such as the social worker. The advocate's case might be that the difference in relationships is due to a difference in competence between the two workers. If only all the professionals were as competent and helpful as the family care worker, his client could keep her child. He might therefore be full of compliments to the family care worker who, not seeing the rest of the case, is pleased she had an easy ride – she does not see the sting in the tail, reserved for the social worker.

Other techniques

There are many other ways of irritating or disconcerting a witness – a patronising or superior attitude can be provocative. The advocate might change styles
from one question to the next, to put the witness off her stride. He might
change pace, or ask quick-fire questions one after another to give the witness
little time to think. Questions and answers take on a rhythm and those
watching end up doing the Wimbledon head movement. Don't allow your pace
to be dictated by the advocate. Just because he is going quickly does not mean
you have to – you do not have to dance to his tune.

At other times, the advocate might introduce long pauses between questions or remain silent when you have finished your answer, implying your
answer is incomplete or making you feel uncomfortable with the silence and
obliged to fill it up. Don't give in to this temptation. If you have finished your
answer, don't say anything else – the ball is in the advocate's court, and the
judge will become impatient if he takes too long before his next question.

Sometimes an advocate might give an exaggerated or dramatic reaction,
raise his eyebrows, or make a great play of noting down your answer in his
book, repeating your words in a questioning or sarcastic tone or saying things
like 'really?' or 'I see' in an apparently significant manner. Alternatively, he may
pretend not to understand your answers. This may mean nothing at all. It may
be designed to unsettle you and make you wonder whether you have just made
a faux pas – it could even be that he is simply playing for time while thinking of
his next question, so do not let it unnerve you.

Advocates are taught not to convey any signal except on purpose. If an
advocate reacts to a response from a witness, it is done deliberately to make a
point to the court or as part of his strategy for handling the witness (unless he is
not very good at his job and cannot contain his own reactions). If something
goes wrong in a case and the answer which emerges has disastrous implications
for his case, the advocate is supposed to 'ride the bumps' and continue to appear
utterly calm and collected as if nothing had happened. This is hopelessly
undermined if, behind him, his client is holding her head in her hands, grimac-
ing, gesticulating or otherwise giving the game away. Remember this in court –
don't undermine your own advocate's efforts if things don't go smoothly in
your case; keep a poker face at all times. The judge does not just look at the
witness box – he sees everyone in court and takes it all in.

Advocates will use to their advantage any errors you may have made,
however minor. This is another reason to double check your statement, as
having the opposing advocate drawing attention even to a small mistake such
as an incorrect date or error in numbering can make you feel a fool and undermine your confidence.

However, don't be afraid of lawyers. Not all advocates are good at their
jobs – like any other profession, some are brilliant, some awful and most are

pretty workmanlike. Even a superb advocate can have a bad day or ask a stupid question – lawyers sometimes get things wrong like everyone else. Don't be perturbed if it seems the opposing advocate isn't very good – you might just be right!

Re-examination

If you feel that all has not gone well for you in cross-examination, remember that your advocate has the chance to re-examine you. This is an opportunity to clarify or correct any points raised in cross-examination or to limit any damage done. If the Children's Guardian is supporting your case, her representative's cross-examination can perform the same function. Remember, in any event, that the whole case does not stand or fall on your performance in the witness box – all the other written and oral evidence is taken into account as well.

After all the local authority witnesses have been called, perhaps the parents' advocate might feel that he has scored some points for his client. His problem, however, is that his next task is to present his own case, including calling his own clients. Frequently, parents' advocates have the experience of feeling quite satisfied with the progress they have made attacking the local authority's case, only to see all their good work undone when their own clients step into the witness box.

To illustrate how these techniques might be put into effect, some examples of cross-examination exchanges taken from real cases appear in Appendix 3.

Frequently asked questions

What if the advocate interrupts me during my answer?

If you look at the judge or magistrates, the advocate cannot stop you just by using eye contact and body language, so he actually has to speak over you. This looks rude, so is not something he does lightly. It is only likely to happen if you are saying something he does not want you to say or if you are rambling in such a long-winded manner that he speaks for everyone in court in trying to shut you up! Assuming it is not the latter, all the more reason for you to plough on and finish what you have to say – after all, you have sworn to tell the whole truth. If the next question is asked before you have finished, simply complete your answer to the first point before going on to the second.

What if my mind goes blank or I just can't speak?

People sometimes think they will be so frozen with fear that they will be unable to utter a single word. In reality this is most unlikely to happen but even if it did, remember that all your evidence is already before the court in your statements. If you do dry up in the witness box, take a moment to refocus. Remind yourself of the child, who is the reason you are there. Count to three and look at your statement to refresh your memory. Take a sip of water, take a deep breath, look at the judge or magistrates and start again.

What if something I say comes out wrong?

Sometimes we get halfway through a sentence and get lost. The best thing to do is stop and start again. If on your mental replay something you have said sounds wrong, or if through a subsequent question it becomes apparent that it has been misunderstood (whether genuinely or deliberately), simply explain to the court that you did not express yourself quite clearly enough and restate what you meant.

I am newly qualified and these are my first care proceedings. Will this be held against me?

This is one of those challenges you can easily anticipate and prepare for. Your qualifications and experience are in your statement so it will be no surprise if the issue is picked up. Don't let it throw you – if your recent qualification is the opposing advocate's best point, he is in trouble! Everyone has to start somewhere and all the professionals in court had a first case once. Having an idea in advance how to respond will help to give you confidence. For a start, you are qualified – recently or not, you have completed a rigorous course of study. Second, you have the advantage that your knowledge is fresh and up to date. Third, your experience is supplemented by that of your supervisor. You also benefit from input from colleagues from your own and other agencies.

Can the advocate ask me personal questions?

You are there as a professional witness and on the whole the court is unlikely to consider personal questions relevant. If you are asked a personal question, the best course of action is politely to raise the issue with the court, not the advocate, and calmly say that as you are there in a professional capacity, you are not sure of the relevance of your personal circumstances to the case.

However, the very nature of social work is such that sometimes questions like whether you have children yourself arise in the course of your work with clients. The court might then expect you to answer the question. If your client has never raised the matter with you, you can legitimately point out that it has never been something which has troubled Mrs X before in your work with her. If, on the other hand, it is a matter you have discussed with the client, then you can explain to the court how you dealt with this.

Some workers are concerned that if they do not have children themselves, this might be seen as a weakness. In fact, it could be just the opposite, as their knowledge is objective not subjective. Besides which, any professional working with children has experience of a far wider range of children than it would be physically possible for any parent to have.

Remember, though, that evidence is a product of events in a case. If you have confided any personal details to a client, she will tell her solicitor and that information is likely to be thrown back at you in court. If you provide ammunition, don't be surprised if it is fired at you. One social worker sympathised with a client, explaining that she too had been through a messy divorce. It was therefore quite predictable that the advocate challenged her in court as to what position she was in to criticise his client's family life when her own life was a mess. If you choose to work in this way, that is a matter for you, but be prepared to find it coming back at you.

There are some pieces of personal information you cannot hide – such as your gender, the colour of your skin, some disabilities, pregnancy or illness (if, for example, you have a lot of sick leave during a case). An advocate might try to argue, for example, that as a white worker you cannot understand the position of his black client, or because you are a woman you have naturally taken the side of the allegedly battered wife against his poor maligned male client. All of these are predictable, if not necessarily very strong, points so you have every opportunity to be prepared for them. The important thing is to keep your cool, explain your objective professionalism and demonstrate it by your reasonable demeanour. You may also wish to acknowledge the client's feelings and tell the court if this is something you have already discussed with her.

What if I am asked for a 'yes' or 'no' answer?

If the answer to the question really is a simple 'yes' or 'no', then do not be afraid to give it. However, in many cases, there are more shades of grey. If the question cannot properly be answered in one word, explain to the court that it is more complicated than the questioner implies and give your fuller answer. Try to avoid saying 'yes, but…' as the advocate will leap in as soon as the word 'yes' has crossed your lips and move on to the next question.

What if the advocate keeps asking me what seems like the same question in different ways?

An advocate might use this technique, perhaps to test out the consistency of your answers, especially if he returns to the question after a gap when he has raised other issues. He is unlikely really to expect a professional witness to change her mind or to be inconsistent, but this does sometimes happen with lay witnesses, whereupon, of course, the advocate pounces on any variation or inconsistency. Alternatively it may be done to unnerve you and make you feel as though you have somehow not given a full or clear enough answer or it might be just to irritate you and make you lose your cool.

All you can do is to keep answering the question and stick to your guns, keeping calm and reasonable at all times. If no one else raises the issue after a while, you might appeal to the court. In one case a psychologist finally said to the judge, 'I really do think I have answered that question' to which the judge said, very emphatically, 'Yes, she has! Several times!'

What if I'm asked a stupid question?

The person asking the question has a right to ask it and is entitled to a response from you. Treat all questions respectfully, whatever you think of them, and do your best to provide an answer. This is especially important for any questions coming from the judge or magistrates. One senior social worker was faced with a question from a magistrate which revealed a lack of the most basic understanding of the issues. The social worker rolled her eyes, looked at the ceiling in overt exasperation, sighed and then proceeded to address the Bench as if they were a group of five-year-olds. Everyone else in court felt embarrassed on her behalf. Whatever you say to your team after court in the privacy of your interview room, never reveal your feelings in court and treat every question coming from the Bench as if it is a privilege to respond to such an insightful enquiry.

Can I be asked about other people's evidence?

You can be asked about evidence given by others, for example, to examine contradictions or inconsistencies between witnesses. If you are the key worker, you should already be familiar with all of the evidence submitted. However, if you are a witness giving a discrete piece of evidence, you may not have seen all the evidence before court, so points raised may come as a surprise to you. Usually, the advocate asks the witness to look at and comment on a particular paragraph in another statement. Always take your time to read it carefully, and also read a paragraph or two before and after to get the point into context. In your answer, make sure you stick to what you can legitimately comment on – you cannot say what another witness saw or thought.

What should I call the judges/magistrates?

Magistrates are collectively called 'Your Worships', and the Chair of the Bench is 'Sir' or 'Madam'. A District Judge is 'Sir' or 'Madam', a Circuit Judge is 'Your Honour' and a High Court Judge is 'My Lord/Lady' or 'Your Lordship/Ladyship'. If you can get this right, it adds to your air of professionalism. One witness knew that she was addressing magistrates, and knew they were 'Your somethings' so came out with 'Your Majesty', which they rather liked! An advocate once went from appearing in the FPC in the morning to the County Court in the afternoon. He accidentally addressed the judge as 'Your Worships', to which the judge replied 'I don't mind being a worship, but I'm not sure that I want to be plural!' If you cannot remember the right form of address, do not get in a stew – just be respectful and the court is unlikely to mind.

What if I get the giggles?

Laughter in court is generally best avoided – courts deal with very serious matters, and humour is out of place. Never try to make a joke when giving evidence. Advocates also attempt humour at their peril. An advocate acting for a parent once thought it appropriate to tell the rottweiler joke as part of his closing submissions (Q. What's the difference between a social worker and a rottweiler? A. You have a chance of getting your child back from a rottweiler), and was met with a deep glowering silence from the Bench. Very occasionally, a lighter moment occurs, or the judge makes a witty remark, greeted by apprecia- tive simpering from all present, but generally it is best to maintain a serious expression.

Sometimes, though, the very fact that we are involved in a solemn occasion where we know that we are not supposed to laugh makes the urge to do so irre- sistible, and this is exacerbated by nerves. We all know that dreadful feeling when something that is not at all funny suddenly becomes the most hilarious thing in the world and the more we try to suppress our giggles, the worse it becomes – known as 'corpsing' in the theatrical world. If you feel the urge to laugh welling up inside you, think of something serious, even upsetting, to get you back in balance. Alternatively focus intensely on a tiny object, such as a speck of dust on a carpet, examine it in minute detail as if meditating to compose yourself. If all else fails, 'accidentally' dropping your pen on the floor gives you an opportunity to hide your face for a moment while you get it back under control.

What if I am sick?

Just having a bit of a cold is not enough to get you out of going to court. If you are genuinely too ill to go, contact your lawyers immediately to discuss what to do – it may, for example, be possible to put your evidence off to another day. You are likely to need a doctor's certificate. It is in fact possible in extreme cir- cumstances for the court to convene around a hospital bed if necessary, so there is no escape!

If you feel ill part way through your evidence, ask for a break, although try to make sure that it does not look like a tactic to avoid difficult questions. On one memorable occasion, when a witness said she felt sick, the judge offered her a bucket!

What if I realise that I know one of the magistrates?

It is crucial to declare this immediately. Justice must not only be done but it must be seen to be done and the court must be utterly impartial. It is possible for the degree of connection between witness and magistrate to be considered. In one case the social worker recognised one of the magistrates as being a member of the same choir. Enquiries established that the two women knew each other only by sight, did not know each other's names and had never spoken. All parties were satisfied that the issue had been aired and agreed that the magistrate could continue to sit. Otherwise, she could have stepped down and the court continued with the two remaining magistrates.

What if there is an important development in the case the night before court?

This is not a TV drama, so you cannot save your revelation until you get into the witness box ('I can now reveal that the abuser is... '). Tell your lawyer immediately, so he can inform the other parties and everyone can consider their position. It may require the filing of further evidence, and possibly an adjournment.

What if I don't personally agree with my authority's recommendation to the court?

This is a matter you must deal with long before the case gets to court. Tell your lawyer straight away so a strategy can be designed. If you wait until you get into the witness box and you are asked for your own professional opinion, you have no option but to answer and to get yourself into all sorts of hot water.

What if there is a break part way through my evidence?

Once you are on oath, you must not discuss the case with anyone until your evidence is finished. If the court breaks for lunch or adjourns until another day before you have finished, you must not talk about the case to anyone unless you have the court's specific permission to do so. This puts you in a lonely position as, of course, you want to ask how you are doing, or what you need to emphasise, but you simply cannot. It is best to stay away from the rest of your team because even if you studiously discuss nothing but the weather, others seeing you will leap to the assumption that you are talking about the case.

Chapter 12

After Court

De-briefing

When the case is over, avoid the temptation to breathe a sigh of relief and rush straight back to the pile of other work you have to do. Always build in time for a full de-briefing along with your senior and your legal team to reflect on the outcome, the process and lessons to take forward to the next case. You may find the questionnaire in Appendix 4 helpful.

Witness feedback

Whenever you give evidence ask for full and honest feedback on how it went. It is quite likely that other people's perceptions will be very different from your own and social workers often tend to believe that they have performed worse than observers think, and find it difficult to accept compliments.

Ask your advocate and any other colleagues who have been in court to give you a detailed review of your evidence – you could ask them to use the witness observation checklist in Appendix 2. If you do not ask, you will not automatically get any feedback at all, especially if you are not the key worker in the case – at most you might receive a standard letter thanking you for coming to court.

Learn from your experience. Build on what went well. Accept praise and acknowledge your strengths – many people perversely seem to find this more difficult than hearing criticisms.

Work on the aspects needing improvement. If things did not go as well as you would have liked, consider where the problem really lies. Was it just an off-day? If so, treat it like falling off a horse; you need to get straight back on. The only way of becoming a better witness is through experience. Get stuck back in as soon as you can so you don't have time to build it into a complex and remember that everyone involved (advocates and judge included) knows what it is like to have a bad day in court – it happens to us all at some time.

Consider whether you could benefit from any mentoring or training on expressing yourself in writing, assertiveness, presentation skills or vocal coaching, or whether you simply need to discuss things with others.

The court's decision

Make sure you properly understand the court's decision, both the full implications of the order itself and the reasons for it. Magistrates tend to hand out their full decisions in writing, so you have a document to consider and can take your time to read it in detail. Judges sometimes do likewise, but often they simply deliver their judgment orally. In this case, it is worth keeping your own notes as you listen, and asking your legal team to provide you with a transcript of the judgment, or at least a typed copy of their notes, as soon as possible, as it is quite difficult to take in the full import of a judgment as it goes along. Take the time to read the judgment closely and analyse the reasons for the decision along with your legal team as there may be significant implications not only for this child and family but for other cases.

In some circumstances it is very important for you to have a copy of the court's order before you leave the building, particularly if you have sought an emergency protection order or recovery order, or in any case where you may swiftly have to show your authority for action.

What if you lose?

By definition, there is a loser in every case; sometimes, although not often, it is the local authority. Of course, it is always disappointing not to get the order you seek – you would not make the application if you did not genuinely believe it to be the right thing – but your job is only to put the case to the court; it is the court's job to decide.

If the decision goes against your authority, there are effectively two choices – appeal, or live with it. The most important thing at an early stage is to put emotion to one side and look dispassionately at the court's decision with your legal advisers. Has the court really got it wrong – are there grounds for appeal? If so, quick action is required as court rules prescribe tight timescales for entering appeals.

Alternatively, was the case actually more finely balanced? Although the outcome was not your preferred one, is it one which you can understand? Could the court in fact have come up with a better solution than the one you were proposing? If so, you need to accept the decision and move on. This of course requires you to reformulate your plans for the child and work with the family; early and anxious consideration within your department is essential. Put aside any resentment about the decision and work earnestly and optimistically to try to make the court's decision work well for the child and family. As this might mean quite a change of direction, it might be time for a change of worker, without any sense of blame or criticism of the original worker. At the same time it is worth considering whether your department could have come up with this solution earlier – is there anything to learn for future cases?

The hardest situation to live with is one where the decision went against you and you feel that it's your fault – if only you and/or your team had performed better, the outcome would have been different and the child is now at continuing risk because of your failure. Natural reactions at this stage might be indulging in 'if only' thinking, blame and recriminations, despair and self-flagellation, denial and deflection or adoption of an ostrich policy, everyone busying themselves with other things and avoiding the subject. None of these reactions help anybody or achieve anything. Difficult though it may be, what is required is a cool-headed, objective analysis. You might need someone who was not directly involved in the case to help with this.

First, it is important to get things into perspective. Don't forget also to consider what went right – even in what feels like a disaster, there are some positives too. When you look at what the problems were, you will probably find that there is no single cause and no single person at fault, but a combination of factors. Don't just consider the court hearing itself – consider the whole process from the social work and inter-agency co-operation before proceedings started right through to the final order.

Don't wallow in failure, but turn it round into a positive learning experience. Consider what needs to change for the future, including any strategic issues for the authority. Make sure the whole department learns the lessons – it is no good if one worker or team learns a hard lesson only to have the same mistake repeated by another team in another case. Having a 'no blame' culture helps people to admit errors and allows everyone to learn from others' mistakes. Remember that successful people and organisations are those who learn from setbacks and emerge stronger for the experience.

Success

In the vast majority of cases, Social Services achieve the outcome they seek. If you 'win' your case, there is clearly cause for satisfaction, although triumphalism is never appropriate. Your objective has been achieved and you can proceed immediately to put your plans for the child into practice.

Take as much time to consider a successful outcome as an unsuccessful one. Feel free to pat yourself on the back and to take credit when it is due. Your lawyers should ensure that senior members of your department are informed of successful outcomes and any complimentary comments made by the court – often criticisms are passed on but compliments are not. Make sure that any positive lessons learned are shared with colleagues and the department as a whole. There is no point in leaving others to re-invent the wheel when you have already done the job. Share with others news of an impressive barrister, an effective expert or techniques that you found worked well for you. Do your bit to counteract the received wisdom that court work is always a traumatic ordeal.

Dealing with the parents

The parents are likely to be in court when the decision is given. Depending on the outcome, they may be angry or distressed. Sometimes they may not understand what the judge says or comprehend its significance. You need to give some thought as to how to deal with the parents' reactions and whether, when and how to approach them.

Remember that, once the proceedings are over, the court, lawyers and Guardian all fade away, leaving the social worker, family and child to pick up the pieces. It is important for you to consider along with your seniors how to resume work with the child and family after court.

Telling the child

Someone has to tell the child what has happened in court. Who should do this and how depends on the child's age, understanding and circumstances. If he has given direct instructions to his solicitor, then that solicitor is the appropriate person to inform him. If not, it may be you or the Guardian, or you may both go together. In any event, liaise with the Guardian and child's solicitor and co-ordinate your approach to ensure that the child receives a consistent message. It is almost certainly not in his best interests to hear from his parents first, so swift action may be needed.

Conclusion

Only the most difficult, serious and intractable cases culminate in court proceedings. The children before the court are the ones whose cases cause the most anxious concern, so any court work must be given utmost priority.

The court arena may be unfamiliar to you, but, when you understand the context in which you are working and how the system works, there should be no mystique to it. Preparing and presenting cases for court is a skill and like any other aspect of your professional practice it takes work and improves with experience. Do not expect it to be easy, but equally do not be intimidated.

The court day is not an isolated event but part of a continuum which starts with the work done by you, your colleagues and other agencies with the child and family concerned. Provided that work is sound, the rest of the task centres on presentation, analysis and explanation, first in your statements, then in oral evidence. Preparation is crucial.

Remember that you are not alone; successful court work depends on co-operation and teamwork. Create and maintain close working relationships, especially with your legal representatives. Make sure you get all the training, advice and support you need.

Once you are in court, never forget that you are there as a professional. The process is not, and must never become, personal. Keep a clear head, and always remember you are there for the child. If you present as a serious, competent, fair and reliable witness you will earn respect not only for yourself but also your profession.

Preparing and presenting evidence to court is a challenging but necessary step in your professional development as a children and families worker. You chose to work in child protection for a reason. You may sometimes question your own sanity for making that choice, but the chances are that you were motivated by the desire to do good and to protect the weak and vulnerable. That is a noble calling, and should not be forgotten in all the day to day difficulties of the work.

As Lord Brown said 'the well-being of innumerable children up and down the land depends crucially upon...social workers concerned with their safety being subjected by the law to but a single duty: that of safeguarding the child's own welfare'.[1]

That is why you do what you do. And that is why you owe it to yourself, your authority, your profession and, above all, the child, to be well prepared the next time someone says to you 'See you in court!'

---

1   *D v East Berkshire Community Health NHS Trust and others* [2005] 2 FLR 284, House of Lords, p.328 [138].

Statement Checklist

Grade the statement from 1 to 5 where 1 = poor, 2 = needs improvement, 3 = average, 4 = good, 5 = excellent

Layout and structure

Complies with court rules	1	2	3	4	5
Looks attractive and easy to read	1	2	3	4	5
Information well organised	1	2	3	4	5
Headings and sub-headings well used	1	2	3	4	5
Paragraphs numbered and sensible length	1	2	3	4	5

Statement writer

Clearly identified	1	2	3	4	5
Role clear	1	2	3	4	5
Expertise established	1	2	3	4	5

Language

Plain English used	1	2	3	4	5
Frank but sensitive	1	2	3	4	5
Professional tone	1	2	3	4	5
Correct spelling and grammar	1	2	3	4	5

Content

Clearly gives key information about child and family	1	2	3	4	5
Special needs/cultural issues considered	1	2	3	4	5
Clear illustrative examples given	1	2	3	4	5
Appropriate level of detail	1	2	3	4	5
Right length and not repetitive	1	2	3	4	5
Addresses both strengths and weaknesses	1	2	3	4	5
Diagrams/exhibits used where helpful	1	2	3	4	5

Hearsay

Use necessary and justification explained	1	2	3	4	5

Opinions and conclusions

Within writer's expertise	1	2	3	4	5
Drawn from facts	1	2	3	4	5
Clearly explained	1	2	3	4	5
Appropriate reference to legal criteria	1	2	3	4	5

Research/theory

Used only where necessary	1	2	3	4	5
Explained clearly and in context of the case	1	2	3	4	5

Overall

Clear	1	2	3	4	5
Balanced and fair	1	2	3	4	5
Professional and reliable	1	2	3	4	5
Inspires confidence in the writer	1	2	3	4	5
Gives the court the information it needs	1	2	3	4	5

Three words which sum up this statement are:

Appendix 2

Witness Observation Checklist

Grade the witness from 1 to 5 where 1 = poor, 2 = needs improvement, 3 = average, 4 = good, 5 = excellent

First impressions

Appearance smart and professional	1	2	3	4	5
Took oath confidently	1	2	3	4	5
Addressed judge/magistrates throughout	1	2	3	4	5
Used correct form of address	1	2	3	4	5

Voice

Clearly audible	1	2	3	4	5
Speech easily understood	1	2	3	4	5
Speed well judged	1	2	3	4	5
Variation of pitch and tone	1	2	3	4	5
Voice calm and assured	1	2	3	4	5

Body language

Composed – neither too relaxed nor too tense	1	2	3	4	5
Gestures natural but not excessive	1	2	3	4	5

Language

Used plain English	1	2	3	4	5
Appropriate level of formality	1	2	3	4	5
Respectful	1	2	3	4	5
Frank but sensitive terminology used	1	2	3	4	5

Evidence

Knowledge of case	1	2	3	4	5
Use of own statement/report	1	2	3	4	5

Responses to questions

Listened carefully to questions	1	2	3	4	5
Asked for repeat of questions if necessary	1	2	3	4	5
Took his/her time	1	2	3	4	5
Answered the question actually asked	1	2	3	4	5
Thoughtful and relevant	1	2	3	4	5
Balanced and fair	1	2	3	4	5
Clear and easily comprehensible	1	2	3	4	5
Answers of appropriate length	1	2	3	4	5
Opinions well explained and justified	1	2	3	4	5
Handled challenges well	1	2	3	4	5
Retained composure under pressure	1	2	3	4	5

Overall

Professional, competent and reliable	1	2	3	4	5
Showed awareness of equal opportunities issues	1	2	3	4	5
Inspired confidence	1	2	3	4	5
Gave the court the information it needed	1	2	3	4	5

Three words which sum up this witness are:

Cross-examination Examples

The following examples are all adapted from exchanges between advocate and witness in real care proceedings cases. The advocate's question is followed in italics by the witness's answer.

In each case, consider what the advocate is trying to achieve and what technique he uses to achieve his objective.

How does the witness handle the questioning? Could she have done anything differently?

What impression does the court gain following these exchanges?

1. Mother's advocate questioning social worker

My client was always in for your visits, wasn't she?
Yes.

And she always let you in?
Yes.

In fact she was quite welcoming, wasn't she?
Yes.

She let you look around her home.
Yes.

And she always allowed you to see the children.
Yes.

She also attended every session of the assessment, didn't she?
Yes.

So my client has been fully co-operative?
Yes.

Commentary

This line of questioning is delivered in a gentle, unchallenging manner and the social worker probably feels relieved at being asked such simple questions. The advocate emphasises the positive aspects of his client's case, leading the witness

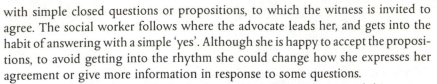

with simple closed questions or propositions, to which the witness is invited to agree. The social worker follows where the advocate leads her, and gets into the habit of answering with a simple 'yes'. Although she is happy to accept the propositions, to avoid getting into the rhythm she could change how she expresses her agreement or give more information in response to some questions.

The problem comes with the final question, which takes a much bigger step than the previous ones and represents a conclusion which is not validly drawn from the preceding information. By now the witness is in the habit of agreeing, so does so again. However, she has made the mistake of agreeing to a proposition which she would not have made herself because, although the mother smilingly attended every session, let workers into her house and pleasantly sat while they spoke she did not actually make any changes or take on board any advice offered. The worker should have considered the last answer more carefully and said something like: 'She is always pleasant and has not been obstructive, but she has not truly co-operated because unfortunately she has not actually made any of the changes we asked her to make.'

As things stand, unless clarification is achieved in re-examination, the advocate has established that Social Services themselves say that his client is fully co-operative. He will use this to support his argument that the children can remain at home because clearly his client will co-operate with any services the local authority wishes to put in to protect them.

2. Mother's advocate questioning social worker in first interim hearing in failure to thrive case

How many previous cases of failure to thrive have you handled?
This is the first.

So you have no previous experience whatsoever of such cases?
No, I'm afraid not, but I am supervised by a senior social worker and the community paediatrician advises me.

Perhaps you can tell the court how many previous cases of failure to thrive your supervisor has handled?
I'm afraid I don't know exactly, but he's very experienced.

You can't tell the court whether he has ever handled a case like this before, can you?
Sorry, no, I can't – but I'm sure he must have.

And does the community paediatrician have any special expertise in failure to thrive?
I'm sure she must have, but I don't really know, sorry – you would have to ask her that.

You didn't think to ask her yourself?
No, I didn't, I'm afraid.

So you can't tell the court that anyone responsible for the case has any special experience or expertise in this area!
I don't know the details, I'm afraid, but I'm sure they must have.

Are you aware of the research into techniques of community management of failure to thrive?
No. I'm sorry.

Commentary

The advocate is obviously seeking to cast doubt on the witness's expertise and at the same time to undermine her confidence – and you may feel that he succeeds. These were the first questions in the cross-examination, so the witness started off shakily and her confidence was undermined for the rest of the session. The worker's inability to provide clear information for the court, coupled with her constant apologies, must have left the magistrates wondering how far they could rely on her as a competent professional.

She could have avoided these problems if she had been able, for example, to outline her theoretical understanding of the issue coupled with details of her senior's practical experience – and she could have reminded the court of her own observations of the baby's condition which in the particular case were such that previous experience was superfluous – it was common sense that something was seriously wrong.

The advocate refers to research. The witness is entitled to ask the court to require him to specify whether he has a particular piece of research in mind. If he proposed to cite this research, he should properly have copied it to other parties in advance. If he has not done so, the witness and her advocate are quite entitled to ask the court for time to read and consider the work he is referring to.

3. Mother's advocate to Children's Guardian supporting an interim care order on a child already voluntarily accommodated in foster care

Why do you support an ICO?
The local authority needs to share parental responsibility.

But my client has never sought to remove the child from accommodation, has she?
No, she hasn't.

And there is no reason to suppose she might do so in future, is there?
No.

In fact my client has confirmed to you that she accepts the child will remain in foster care for the time being, hasn't she?
Yes, she has.

So an interim care order would add nothing, would it?
It would mean the local authority would share parental responsibility.

On a day to day basis precisely what difference would that make?
It would make things more secure, and put the local authority in charge.

Forgive me, I was asking in practical terms on a day to day basis, precisely what difference it would make?
The local authority would have parental responsibility and it would secure the child where he is.

The reality is, isn't it, that it you cannot tell the court of one single practical difference it would make, can you! Moving on…

Commentary

In these answers, the Guardian repeats that 'the local authority would have parental responsibility' like a mantra – but it seems she has given little thought to what, if any, real difference it would make. She speaks in generalities and abstractions, when the questions ask for practicalities, so she fails to answer the questions asked, leading to the inference that she has no answer.

Obviously the advocate's questions lead towards submissions on the 'no order' principle and the doctrine of proportionality. He has established that his client has not tried to remove the child, nor is there any suggestion she will do so, she has agreed he will remain in foster care without an order, and no practical reason has been given for an order. Not surprisingly, no order was granted. Never apply for or support an order if you cannot tell the court in plain terms why it is needed.

4. Mother's advocate to social worker in interim care order application

You apply for an interim care order?
Yes, the department's view is that it is now necessary to seek an interim care order with a view to removing the children from home.

Do you agree that children should only be removed from home when absolutely necessary and as a last resort?
Of course.

Do you think that removal is absolutely necessary in this case?
The department takes the view that it is.

I didn't ask what the department thinks. I asked what you think. You are a professional, so what is your own professional opinion?
I have to say that I don't agree that it is necessary.

Commentary

This was a painful personal experience the recollection of which still causes a shudder, many years later! The social worker and her senior had omitted to tell the legal department that there was a stark difference of professional views and that the key worker disagreed with the application to the court. That same worker was the only witness representing the department in making the application, which, unbeknown to her lawyer, she did not personally support.

The opposing advocate picked up on the worker's consistent reference in her answers to 'the department' and guessed that she was trying to distance herself from the decision. Once the worker was asked the final question, she had little option. She was there as a representative of the department and had made its position clear. However, she was also there as a professional witness and when pressed for her own professional judgment, she clearly could not lie on oath. She therefore gave the only answer she could – to her own lawyer's dismay! You can imagine how far the interim care order application progressed after that.

Court is not the place to tackle professional disagreements. It is neither sensible nor kind to shock your own lawyer in court. If these issues arise, they must be tackled in advance and in conjunction with your legal team – please!

5. Mother's solicitor to social worker

You complain that my client is rude to you?
That's correct, she does not listen to my advice and is often abusive.

You're newly qualified aren't you?
I have been fully professionally qualified for nine months. I hardly think that's newly qualified, and I have gained considerable experience in that time.

Really? Considerable experience in nine months?
Yes. Absolutely.

You haven't got children yourself have you?
I consider that irrelevant and decline to answer that question.

Even assuming you have some theoretical knowledge, you have no idea what it's like for my client trying to cope on her own with three children under five, do you?
I use the benefit of my professional expertise in working with this mother.

Are you aware that my client finds you unsympathetic and unhelpful?
She has made that perfectly clear many times.

Is it any wonder she sometimes loses her patience and swears at you?
Verbal abuse is not justified whatever her feelings towards me.

Commentary

This advocate clearly knows he cannot refute evidence that his client has failed to co-operate with the social worker and has been abusive to her. His approach is, therefore, to seek to explain his client's actions by showing her feelings about the social worker to be understandable, if not entirely justified. You may consider that the tone of the worker's answers, even referring to 'this mother' rather than using her name, only serves to assist him in this endeavour. If the worker had seemed more understanding of his client's difficulties or shown some empathy towards her, his strategy would have been difficult to sustain. As it is, he is on his way to establishing that the worker is inexperienced, unsympathetic, judgemental and defensive.

He hopes that later when his client gives evidence she will cut a sympathetic figure, preferably apologising for her rudeness to the social worker – then in submissions he will appeal to the Bench effectively saying, 'No wonder things didn't improve – my poor client didn't stand a chance given this obnoxious social worker.'

6. Mother's advocate to expert medical witness

Is it possible that the injuries could have been caused by another child?
Well, they were inflicted by someone. It is not possible to determine the age of the perpetrator from the injuries, the only rough guide might come from looking at the force required to cause the injuries. They could have been caused by a child, depending on the age of child you have in mind.

A two-year-old?
Oh no, definitely not! That's simply not possible – only a much older child or an adult could have the strength to inflict injuries of this severity.

Commentary

This advocate's case theory is that the injuries were not caused by his clients but by another child, aged two. However, he overplays his hand. One of the key skills of advocacy is knowing when to stop and to refrain from asking that one question too many. Here, if he had stopped after the first question, his case theory would still be intact – he could tell the court there is an alternative explanation for the injuries, which is plausible because the expert said so. Unfortunately for him, he goes too far and by trying to get the confirmation of the detail of his hypothesis, he succeeds only in destroying it. Sometimes advocates simply get it wrong.

End of Case Questionnaire

(Where ratings are suggested from 1 to 5, 1 = poor, 2 = needs improvement, 3 = average, 4 = good, 5 = excellent)

Outcome

What was the outcome?

. . . .

Was it as expected?   Y / N

Working relationships

How effective was the relationship between Social   1   2   3   4   5
Services and legal representatives?

What was the most successful aspect of the relationship?

. . . .

What was the least successful?

. . . .

How effective was co-operation with other agencies?   1   2   3   4   5

What was the most successful element of co-operation?

. . . .

What was the least successful?

. . . .

How constructive was the relationship with the
Children's Guardian?   1   2   3   4   5

Why?

. . . .

. . . .

Court procedures

Did case administration work smoothly?   Y / N

Were all court deadlines complied with?   Y / N

If not, where did the problems lie?

....

....

....

Evidence

How well prepared were the local authority's witness
statements?   1   2   3   4   5

What were their strengths?

....

....

....

What could be improved upon?

....

....

....

How effective were the local authority's witnesses in
court?   1   2   3   4   5

What were their strengths?

....

....

....

What could be improved upon?

....

....

....

Expert

Was the report delivered on time?	Y / N
How useful was it?	1 2 3 4 5
How effective was the expert as a witness in court?	1 2 3 4 5
Would you use this expert again?	Y / N

Give your reasons:

. . . .

. . . .

. . . .

Advocates

How helpful was the local authority's advocate in conference, case preparation and negotiations?	1 2 3 4 5
How effective was he/she in court?	1 2 3 4 5
Would you use this advocate again?	1 2 3 4 5

Give your reasons:

. . . .

. . . .

. . . .

Were any of the other advocates impressive?	Y / N
Would you like to instruct them in another case?	Y / N

Overall

What worked well in the case?

. . . .

. . . .

. . . .

Would you do anything differently next time?

. . . .

. . . .

. . . .

What have you learned from the case?

. . . .

. . . .

. . . .

What lessons from the case (positive messages or suggestions for improvement) should be shared with social work or legal colleagues, or with other agencies?

. . . .

. . . .

. . . .

Further Resources

www.hmcourts-service.gov.uk	Information about courts
www.judiciary.gov.uk	Information about the judiciary
www.jsboard.co.uk	Information about judicial training
www.dca.gov.uk	Department for Constitutional Affairs site
www.lawsociety.org.uk	Includes list of Children Panel solicitors
www.barcouncil.org.uk	Barristers' professional body website
www.family-justice-council.org.uk	Includes research section
www.cafcass.gov.uk	Information about children's Guardians
www.nagalro.com	Guardians' site including information About research
www.alc.org.uk	Association of Lawyers for Children site
www.plainenglish.org.uk	For guidance on plain English
www.suzylamplugh.org.uk	For information on personal safety

Truss, L. (2005) *Eats, Shoots & Leaves – The Zero Tolerance Approach to Punctuation.* London: Profile Books.

Index